PRAISE FOR
Jazzy Vegetarian Classics

"*Jazzy Vegetarian Classics* brings vegan comfort food mainstream in a very accessible way. Who doesn't love comfort food? Dishes always taste even better when they are cruelty free!"
— Emily Deschanel, star of Fox TV's hit show *Bones*

"I love this cookbook—tasty twists on classic American cuisine. Vegan cooking is neither boring nor tasteless, and the Jazzy Vegetarian proves it again and again with the recipes in this book. I love it!"
—Belinda Carlisle

"*Jazzy Vegetarian Classics* is a stunning masterpiece exemplifying how decadent a healthy, plant-based diet can be. Laura Theodore exudes jazzy passion and beauty that will inspire you to love being in the kitchen."
—Julieanna Hever, MS, RD, CPT, author of *The Complete Idiot's Guide to Plant-Based Nutrition* and host of "What Would Julieanna Do?"

"Who knew vegan treats could be so scrumptious! Anyone who's tasted Laura Theodore's food knows. Try her new amazing dishes . . . with a twist!"
—Ed Begley, Jr., actor, director, and environmentalist

"Laura Theodore does it again by creating easy, accessible, and tasty recipes that are also healthy. *Jazzy Vegetarian Classics* is a must have for anyone wanting to expand their repertoire of great tasting dishes that remind you of Mom's cooking. And my favorite part—you won't have to go to some specialty market to find the ingredients, most of them are available in your neighborhood grocery store."
—Chef Del Sroufe, author of *Forks Over Knives—The Cookbook* and *Better Than Vegan*

"Whether you're a part-time vegetarian or a seasoned vegan, you'll adore Laura Theodore's healthy twists on classic American dishes. From twice-baked potatoes oozing with a creamy (and good-for-you) filling to a to-die-for black forest pecan pie that will dazzle any guest, your family gatherings will never be the same. In her typical fashion, Laura infuses wisdom and helpful cooking tips into every recipe, and has once again made plant-based food accessible, innovative, and delicious."
—Colleen Holland, Co-Founder of *VegNews Magazine*

"*Jazzy Vegetarian Classic*s is packed with fresh ideas on preparing delicious, healthy, plant-based recipes. This book gives you everything you need to plan a satisfying meal from salad through dessert, and even select music to enhance your eating pleasure. Laura Theodore's positive energy shines through every page, making this a fun read sure to inspire you to eat more whole foods—and enjoy every bite of it."
—Janice Stanger, PhD, author of *The Perfect Formula Diet*

"*Jazzy Vegetarian Classics* is a much needed cookbook, as it will make healthful, delicious vegan cuisine accessible and approachable for one and all. Looking at the beautiful photos makes me want to cook and invite others over for an amazing, healthful, and delicious meal. Laura is a living example of what she believes in. The dishes are simple, nutritious, and easy to prepare. It is a blessing that Laura Theodore is providing healthful, conscious options so that we all may enjoy classic American favorites with an eye toward health and vitality."
—Gurmukh Kaur Khalsa, internationally renowned Kundalini yoga teacher, founder of Golden Bridge Yoga, and author of *The Eight Human Talents* and *Bountiful, Beautiful, Blissful*

"More and more people are interested in exploring healthful, vegan cuisine, and the *Jazzy Vegetarian Classics* cookbook is making it fun and easy. Eating plants instead of animals has never been so enjoyable."
—Gene Baur, President and Co-Founder of Farm Sanctuary

"The genius of *Jazzy Vegetarian Classics* is that the recipes magically transform incredibly healthy vegetarian ingredients into extraordinary family classics much better than the original. The book promises those who indulge not only fabulous meals, but also a wonderfully healthy life. Nature's path toward vegetarianism has never been so easy to follow!"
—Daniel A. Nadeau, MD, author of *The Color Code: A Revolutionary Eating Plan for Optimum Health*

Jazzy Vegetarian Classics

VEGAN TWISTS

on

AMERICAN FAMILY FAVORITES

LAURA THEODORE

BenBella Books
Dallas, TX

BenBella

BenBella Books, Inc.
10300 N. Central Expressway, Suite 530
Dallas, TX 75231
www.benbellabooks.com
Send feedback to feedback@benbellabooks.com

Printed in the United States of America
10 9 8 7 6 5 4 3 2 1

Library of Congress Cataloging-in-Publication Data

Theodore, Laura.
    Jazzy vegetarian classics : vegan twists on American family favorites / by Laura Theodore.
        pages   cm
    Includes bibliographical references and index.
    ISBN 978-1-937856-93-9 (hardback) — ISBN 978-1-937856-94-6 (electronic)
    1. Vegan cooking—United States.   2. Cooking, American.   I. Title.
    TX837.T455   2013
    641.5'636—dc23   2013012312

Cover photo by Joe Orecchio
Hair and makeup by Victoria De Los Rios
Interior photos by Andy Ebberbach, Peter
    Capozzi, and David Kaplan
Interior photos on pages xiii, xx, 16, 40, 116,
    162, 184, and 274 by Joe Orecchio
Interior photos on pages viii, 62, 70, and 231 by
    Meghan Capozzi Rowe
Full cover design by Sarah Dombrowsky

Front cover design by Kit Sweeney
Editing by Trish Sebben-Krupka, Debbie
    Harmsen, and Vy Tran
Copyediting by Shannon Kelly
Proofreading by Cape Cod Compositors, Inc.,
    and Kimberly Marini
Text design and composition by Kit Sweeney
    and Ralph Fowler
Printed by Bang Printing

Distributed by Perseus Distribution
(www.perseusdistribution.com)

To place orders through Perseus Distribution:
Tel: (800) 343-4499
Fax: (800) 351-5073
E-mail: orderentry@perseusbooks.com

Significant discounts for bulk sales are available. Please contact Glenn Yeffeth at glenn@benbellabooks.com or (214) 750-3628.

Jazzy Vegetarian gratefully acknowledges our sponsors,
Tropicana, Quaker, Vitamix, and Dawn,
whose generous support has made it
possible to share these recipes
with the world.

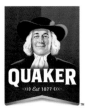

MY MISSION

Making the world a better place,
one recipe at a time.

Contents

Easy Vegan Paella (page 180)

Foreword

For eighteen years, I've helped people all over the world to understand the relationship between diet and health and that eating a well-structured plant-based diet can prevent, stop, and even reverse some degenerative diseases. My job gets easier every year—more and more people are interested in plant-based eating because they care about health, the environment, and protecting animals. But my job is also easier because of talented individuals like Laura Theodore, who can make plant-based eating an extraordinary experience.

Laura is not just a competent cook or a good singer; she is a fabulous chef and a consummate entertainer who inspires people to want to eat good food not because it's healthy, but because it tastes and looks fabulous. On her television show and in this book, she entices people, regardless of their current eating habits, to want to explore new foods and dishes. Her passion for food, music, and the art of presentation is contagious.

Jazzy Vegetarian Classics shows people who enjoy food that they are not giving up anything by eating more healthfully, but rather entering a world where food is more interesting, varied, and delicious. The recipes are not just for vegetarians or vegans, but for anyone who loves and celebrates food.

Hippocrates said, "Let food be thy medicine," and Laura Theodore makes the medicine taste oh-so-good!

Pamela A. Popper, PhD, ND
Founder and President,
The Wellness Forum

Acknowledgments

I would like to express my heartfelt gratitude to all of my dear family and friends who have continually given me their unconditional love, pleased palates, and gracious support for my plant-based life path.

First and foremost, I'd like to thank Andy, my partner in life and husband of 23 years, who has been a devoted taste-tester for all of the recipes in this book and many more.

My deep appreciation goes to Regina Eisenberg, Dave Davis, Cheri Arbini, Pat Kruis, Dr. Pam Popper, Peter Capozzi, and John Capozzi. This project would not have been possible without their talent, guidance, hard work, and continued support and belief in the Jazzy Vegetarian concept.

My gratitude goes to my fabulous editor, Trish Sebben-Krupka, for helping me to achieve my vision and for her creative talent and great patience in editing this book. Thank you to Glenn Yeffeth, Debbie Harmsen, Adrienne Lang, Monica Lowry, Vy Tran, Kit Sweeney, Lindsay Marshall, Jennifer Canzoneri, Leigh Camp, and everyone at BenBella Books for their hard work to make this book achievable.

I am grateful to my multitalented sous chef and kitchen wizard, Alicia McMahon, along with the rest of our talented television crew, especially our "A" cameraman, David Kaplan, and gaffer Jeff Pacailler. Many thanks also to my makeup artists, Victoria De Los Rios and Keira Karlin, and hair designers, Andrea Senatore and Kym Rebelo.

My deep appreciation goes to the vegan and vegetarian cookbook authors, nutritionists, and physicians who have shared their thoughts and ideas throughout the years. Much love and many thanks go to my beautiful, talented, and incredible girlfriends for taste-testing and sharing thoughts about many of the recipes in this book.

In addition, my admiration goes to all of the hardworking farmers that I have had the great opportunity to meet and learn from during the past eight years.

And a big thank you goes to *the animals*. This cookbook is for you.

Chickpea and Quinoa Salad in Sweet Pepper Boats
(page 143)

Jazzylicious Shish Kebabs
(page 176)

Lovely Lemon Cake
(page 242)

"Nothing will benefit human health and increase chances for survival of life on Earth as much as the evolution to a vegetarian diet."

—Albert Einstein

Introduction

For me, plant-based cooking is like singing jazz: making creative and spicy improvisations with a delicious twist! As a jazz singer, I love scatting a new phrase to enhance a classic song, so when I cook, I savor the process of improvising new versions of traditional recipes, depending on what's in my kitchen or available at the local market—or on what it's being paired with for a complete meal. Having this jazzy approach to cooking influenced me when I first started eating a plant-based diet, helping me to create fabulous vegan meals that reflected the tastes and textures of timeless American recipes.

In the pages of this book, my goal is to help others have fun in the kitchen with easy-to-prepare meals. On my television show, *Jazzy Vegetarian*, I adore merging my love for plant-based recipes with my love of music, sharing my creative but laid-back approach to cooking, and serving up some jazzy tunes on the side!

How It Began

I always knew I wanted to be singer and actor when I grew up. The desire was something I seem to have been born with. When I was three, my paternal grandfather was attempting to film my beautiful baby sister, Julie, as she posed on a baby blanket. Instead, what you mostly see in the clip is me wildly singing and dancing for the camera, performing what looks to be a very wayward Shirley Temple routine. On the other hand, one of my first fond memories is of me about that same age, standing on a stool in my maternal grandmother's kitchen, stirring apples for her yearly batch of applesauce. It seemed that there were apples everywhere—on the counters, in baskets on the floor, apples simmering in a huge pot on the stove, cooked apples in a bowl, and apples being put through a hand-cranked mill that helped to grind up the apple skins.

I always *loved* food and I remember being fascinated when my mom took beautifully cooked artichokes out of the pot, or when my great aunt came to visit and made homemade pasta noodles. On Sundays or holidays, I looked forward to entering my maternal Grandma Cook's kitchen. (Yes, Cook was her real last name!) It was always filled with the intoxicating aroma of a big pot of simmering spaghetti sauce or some other wonderful culinary creation that she was preparing for us to feast upon.

Fast forward to my teen years, when I had very little interest in cooking, but I certainly loved eating! My focus then was on studying the art of acting, dancing, and singing, and I performed regularly in musicals on stage and television. However, when it came time for me to move out of the house, I realized if I was going to eat great home-cooked food, I needed to actually learn to cook!

Almost weekly, my grandmother mailed her recipes to me. My mother often sent recipes too, so I began collecting them and storing them in a little recipe box. I became interested in the science of food and started experimenting with these cherished family recipes, making them my own. Several years later, I became interested in becoming a vegetarian and so I started converting the recipes into vegetarian versions by substituting ingredients like tofu for cheese or grains for meat.

Five years passed. As a professional actor and recording artist residing and working in New York City, I began entertaining my fellow musicians and actors off the stage by serving my sweet and savory vegetarian feasts to a constantly appreciative crowd. That got me thinking about how to merge my musical and culinary skills into one.

I was a big fan of all of the popular cooking shows that were emerging on television but a bit chagrined that none of them focused on vegan cuisine. I dreamed that someday I would have my own innovative cooking show. By sharing my plant-based culinary creations on the small screen, I could prove to viewers across America and beyond how easy it is to cook sans animal products—and how totally delicious the results are! When my husband and I started brainstorming titles for the show, we laughed hysterically when we came up with the name *Jazzy Vegetarian*. Catchy, we thought, but was it too radical to use the word *vegetarian* in the title? This was many years ago, when the word vegetarian was still considered to be a bit taboo.

We went with it because it was not only catchy, but also fitting. The jazzy part of the title is my secret ingredient—me sharing my love of singing a catchy tune with my passion for cooking. The vegetarian part relates to what I love to cook—great vegan food.

Vegetarian vs. Vegan

Since all of my recipes are vegan, people ask me why I am the Jazzy Vegetarian and not the Jazzy Vegan. Well, when we were thinking of names, we wondered if most people even knew what a vegan was. Back then, it wasn't part of the common vernacular. In fact, it was almost like a dirty word. Boy, have times changed!

Recently I did a little online research about the histories and origins of the words vegetarian and vegan. According to the Vegetarian Society of the United Kingdom, the practice of vegetarianism was more commonly known as "the vegetable diet" before the word *vegetarian* was officially coined in conjunction with the formation of the society in 1847. It comes from the Latin word *vegetus*, meaning invigorating, lively, vivid, active, or energetic. The members of the Vegetarian Society who adapted the word emphasized and sought to spread a message of good health and moral responsibility through vegetarianism, so the original meaning of the word implies a lot more than just a diet of vegetables and fruit.

In fact, according to John Davis, who is a pioneer of vegetarianism on the Internet and a trustee of the Vegetarian Society of the UK, the first people who called themselves "vegetarian" were actually vegan. Some historians believe that until 1847 all uses of the word vegetarian came from people associated with Alcott House School, an institution southwest of London started by a radical educator, and they used it to indicate individuals who consumed a 100 percent plant-based food diet. In other words, a vegetarian simply meant someone who "lived on vegetation."[1]

The term *vegan* did not exist independently of vegetarianism for another 100 years, when Donald Watson, cofounder of the Vegan Society, coined it in 1944. According to Watson, he wanted a concise word to replace "nondairy vegetarian," so he derived "vegan" from the first three and last two letters of "vegetarian"— "the beginning and end of vegetarian." [2]

So, in fact, the Jazzy Vegetarian *is* vegan!

What does the word vegan mean to me? Well, here is the way I see it: A vegan is someone who does not use or consume any meat, poultry, fish, dairy, or eggs. A vegan strives to eat a purely plant-based diet consisting of fruits, vegetables, seeds, legumes, nuts, and grains. That's what my recipes are all about: plant-based, easy-to-prepare, and delicious!

A Plant-Based Diet

Folks often ask me, "Laura, what inspired you to focus on a purely plant-based way of eating?" My personal reasons for embracing a vegan diet are threefold: my compassion for animals, my desire for better health, and my aim to be more environmentally responsible. You may have your own reasons for learning more about plant-based cooking, so I thank you, in advance, for joining me on this creative culinary path. Whether you are a dedicated vegan, or just looking to add a few plant-based recipes into your weekly menu plan, I invite you to explore the pages of this book. It's meant to both entertain and inspire, while encouraging you to create signature recipes in your own home kitchen.

So whether we use the term vegetarian, vegan, or plant-based to describe the recipes in this book, we are all talking about the same thing—recipes based on fruits, vegetables, seeds, legumes, nuts, and whole grains that are compassionate, nutritious, and great tasting! Together we can make the world a better place to live in, one jazzylicious recipe at a time!

Happy, Healthy Cooking!

---

[1] www.vegsource.com/john-davis/vegetarian-equals-vegan.html

[2] www.vegparadise.com/24carrot610.html

Jazzylicious Shish Kebabs (page 176)

Chapter 1

The Jazzy Basics

There are some fundamental foods, tools, and, well, basically "basics" that are essential in my daily cooking. They make my life in the kitchen easier and a lot more fun. I'll bet ease and fun are things you'd like to have in your kitchen, too, so in this chapter I share some of my favorites with you. Let's get cookin'!

"I'll play it first and tell you
what it is later."

——Miles Davis

Glossary of Ingredients

Here, you'll find a comprehensive list of some of the star ingredients featured in this book. The good news is that most of these items are found in major supermarkets nationwide. If your grocer does not currently carry an item you are looking for, try asking the store manager to order the item specifically for you. I have had great luck with this tactic, leading to the item being regularly stocked in the store.

Brown rice (short grain, long grain, basmati): Brown rice comes in both short- and long-grain varieties and may be the most commonly used grain in vegan cooking. Brown rice has a slightly nutty flavor and is chewier and more nutritious than refined white rice. Brown rice is delicious either served by itself as a side dish with vegetables and beans, or as a basic ingredient in casseroles and soups. Brown rice can easily become rancid when stored at room temperature, so refrigerate it after purchase.

Brown sugar, vegan: Pure brown sugar has a distinctive molasses flavor that enhances many recipes, giving them a sweet, rich flavor. It is especially tasty in homemade baked goods or sprinkled over hot cereals. I like to buy organic, fair-trade brown sugar whenever possible. To be sure your brown sugar is vegan, purchase a brand that has been made without the use of any animal products during the manufacturing process. Several vegan-friendly sugar companies are listed online.

Cheese, vegan: This "cheese" is easily substituted for dairy cheese in most recipes, and a wide variety of flavors and styles are usually available in supermarkets and health food stores. If you are looking for a vegan cheese, be sure it is free of casein or calcium caseinate (a milk protein that may be used in soy protein cheeses for texture). There are many tasty rice, pea protein, soy, tapioca starch, arrowroot, and even hemp-based vegan cheeses in the marketplace today. Vegan cheese is delicious in sandwiches (both cold and grilled), lasagna, casseroles, and even cubed and served as a snack on a whole-grain cracker.

Cocoa powder, unsweetened: Cocoa powder is made by grinding cacao beans and pressing out the cocoa butter, resulting in a dense powder that's low in fat but high in flavor. It adds a rich and flavorful chocolate taste to recipes such as baked goods and puddings. Try buying organic, fair-trade nonalkalized cocoa powder whenever it is available, and read the label to be sure it's dairy-free!

Dark chocolate, vegan: Good-quality dark chocolate is made by adding sugar and fat (typically cocoa butter) to ground cacao beans, the seeds from cacao (chocolate) trees. For a vegan option, purchase chocolate that is fair-trade, organic, and dairy-free. Today, there are many nondairy varieties of dark chocolate readily available in most major supermarkets. For a deep, rich taste, purchase dark chocolate that is labeled as containing at least 60 percent or higher cacao content.

Extra-virgin olive oil: Olive oil is a rich and flavorful fruit oil obtained from olives. The International Olive Oil Council (IOOC) defines extra-virgin olive oil as oil coming from cold pressing of the olives, containing no more than 0.8 percent acidity, and having a superior flavor. I use it sparingly, but extra-virgin olive oil can be tasty when used in salad dressings or to add extra flavor to casseroles, soups, sauces, stews, baked goods, or lightly sautéed vegetables.

Flaxseeds (golden or brown), freshly ground: Freshly ground flaxseeds are high in lignans, which are touted to have a host of health benefits. Freshly ground flaxseeds have an impressive omega-3 fatty acid content, and they are high in both soluble and insoluble fiber. Found in most health food stores and some supermarkets, golden flaxseeds work well in baking and smoothie recipes, and they are also tasty sprinkled on cereals or salads. Before using the flaxseeds, grind them with a high-performance blender or grain mill. If you don't have either of those, use a coffee grinder you've designated for flaxseeds only.

Gomasio: *Gomasio* is a dry condiment made from unhulled sesame seeds. *Gomasio* can be enhanced with flavorings such as sea salt, seaweed, or garlic to name a few. Sprinkle *gomasio* over steamed veggies, stews, pasta dishes, or soups right before serving to add flavor and texture. Look for *gomasio* in the Asian ingredients aisle of your grocery store.

Maple sugar: Maple sugar is produced by boiling pure maple syrup in order to concentrate the sugars. As it cools, it is stirred from a liquid solution into pure maple granulated sugar. You can substitute ⅔ cup of maple sugar in most recipes for 1 cup of brown sugar. Maple sugar is delicious sprinkled over hot oatmeal or stirred into fresh lemonade. I often use it in cookies, muffins, cakes, and other dessert recipes. It adds a sweet flavor to steamed carrots, baked squash, sweet potatoes, or even marinara sauce!

Maple syrup: Maple syrup is a sweet, sugary-tasting syrup made from the sap extracted from various types of maple trees. Purchase organic maple syrup whenever it is available to avoid undesirable additives. I cook with Grade B maple syrup, which is darker in color and thicker in consistency than the Grade A variety, so it delivers a more concentrated maple flavor. If you prefer a lighter maple taste, buy the Grade A variety, which is lighter in color and has a less intense flavor profile.

Margarine, vegan: Vegan margarine is often sold as a tub-style spread. It can be substituted for stick butter or margarine in most any recipe. Buy a vegan margarine that is non-GMO (free of genetically modified ingredients), organic, and free of hydrogenated oils, and use it sparingly. Spread it on baked goods or cook with it in any recipe that calls for butter or margarine.

Marinara sauce, vegan: A good, low-fat, jarred marinara makes a time-saving staple for many plant-based recipes such as lasagna, chili, sauces, casseroles, stews, and more. Opt for jarred rather than canned marinara to avoid a metallic taste. Read the label to make sure there are no dairy or meat products used in the brand that you choose. Keep several jars stocked in your pantry for use when time is at a premium.

Mayonnaise, vegan: Egg-free vegan mayonnaise can be used in place of traditional mayonnaise in most recipes. It is often soy-, safflower-, or grapeseed-based, and it is now also available in low-fat varieties. Found in health food stores and many supermarkets, this mayonnaise-style spread is usually displayed in either the refrigerated section or the condiment aisle. Vegan mayonnaise is perfect to use in pasta or potato salad or as a base for homemade dips and salad dressings.

Medjool dates: The medjool date is the fruit of the date palm tree. There are many varieties of dates, but medjool dates are generally larger and sweeter, so they are ideal to use in baked goods and desserts. I prefer medjool dates over other varieties because they are very soft and quite sweet. On their own, they make a great snack. Plus, I like adding pitted dates to smoothies to sweeten them up naturally. Yum!

Nondairy milk: Nondairy milk, such as soy, almond, rice, oat, hemp, coconut, cashew, or hazelnut milk, is now readily found in supermarkets and health food stores nationwide. Organic, nonflavored, plant-based milks make the perfect substitute for dairy milk in most recipes. The flavored and sweetened varieties are ideal for use in smoothies or baking, pouring over cereal, or just plain sipping!

Nori (toasted sheets): Nori is one of the tastiest sea vegetables. Good quality nori has a sweet, delicate flavor and is a good source of minerals, vitamins, iodine, and protein. Use toasted nori sheets for making sushi or nori rolls, or grind them in a blender and then sprinkle the powder in salads or soups. A bonus: nori is fat-free, low-sodium, and a source of calcium.

Quinoa: This excellent alternative to brown rice is technically a seed, not a grain, but its texture, taste, and preparation method echoes that of many whole grains, so it is often categorized as a grain. Quinoa is quick to prepare (it cooks up in 15 to 17 minutes) and is high in protein. Quinoa is thought to be a "complete" protein due to the presence of balanced proportions of all nine essential amino acids. Quinoa is delightful when used as a stuffing for peppers or squash, and it is delicious served alongside a healthy-sized plate of steamed vegetables or cooked up with canned beans to make a quick and hearty supper. Cooked quinoa makes a great base for a cold summer salad or a tasty thickener for soups.

Salsa: There are many varieties of jarred salsa available in most health food stores and supermarkets. Salsa can be tomato-, vegetable-, or fruit-based. Salsa can be mild and sweet tasting, hot and spicy, or anything in between. Some tasty salsa flavors include tomato, mango, pineapple, and chipotle. Keep jars of salsa stocked in your pantry, as they can be used to enhance recipes such as chili or soup, used as a quick topper for baked potatoes, or simply poured in a bowl and served with dippers such as whole-grain tortilla chips or veggie sticks. Try to buy salsa that is labeled as being both organic and low-fat.

Seitan: Seitan is made from wheat and is otherwise known as "wheat meat." Seitan is high in protein and it becomes surprisingly similar to meat in appearance, flavor, and texture when cooked, making it a popular meat substitute for many vegans. Although not as common a meat substitute as tofu, seitan is quickly gaining popularity, particularly in vegetarian restaurants. Seitan can be prepared by hand using either whole-wheat flour or vital wheat gluten. I adore using seitan in meatless loafs, meatless burgers, shish kebabs, and oil-free sautés.

Prepared seitan can be found in the refrigerated section of most health food stores and some supermarkets.

Tahini (sesame): Tahini is made by grinding hulled or unhulled sesame seeds into a creamy paste. Tahini is rich in calcium and it has a texture similar to peanut butter, but its taste is a bit milder and less sweet. Tahini is traditionally used in hummus (a tasty dip made from mashed chickpeas, flavored with lemon juice and garlic), but it is also delightful used in cookies, pie crusts, and salad dressings. Tahini is available in jars or cans, and it can be found in health food stores or in the ethnic food section of most supermarkets.

Tamari, reduced-sodium: Tamari sauce is rich and mellow-tasting, with a more complex flavor profile than ordinary soy sauce. Since it is fermented naturally, its flavor is more delicate than that of conventional soy sauce. Tamari has subtle flavor-enhancing properties that pair well with many recipes. The reduced-sodium version has about 25 percent less sodium than regular tamari, and you can use it as a substitute for table salt. For every ¼ teaspoon of sea salt (about 590 mg of sodium) listed in a recipe, replace it with about 1 teaspoon of reduced-sodium tamari (about 233 mg of sodium). Make sure to buy tamari that has been made with GMO-free soybeans, is MSG-free, and contains no artificial preservatives. Gluten-free tamari is also available. Use tamari as a flavor booster in sauces, casseroles, pasta dishes, and vegan gravies. It pairs beautifully in stir-fries, with steamed vegetables, and in soups to help create a smooth but full flavor. It also adds great flavor to both sweet and savory marinades for tofu, tempeh, mushrooms, or squash.

Tempeh (non-GMO): Tempeh is made from the controlled fermentation of soybeans. There are many tasty varieties available, such as five-grain tempeh (can be made with soybeans, brown rice, millet, barley, and rye) or three-grain tempeh (can be made with soybeans, plus brown rice, barley, and millet). Tempeh comes in cakes or patties, making it an ideal meat substitute in many recipes. It has a very mild mushroom-like flavor that is slightly chewy in texture, and it readily absorbs marinades. Tempeh is great used in sandwiches, casseroles, stews, and soups. Try tempeh lightly steamed and served on top of steamed veggies or a crisp green salad. Always buy non-GMO, organic tempeh from a reputable source. Once you get the hang of cooking with tempeh, you'll want to make it a staple of your regular diet.

Tofu (non-GMO): This versatile soy food has been a popular mainstay in vegetarian and vegan diets for decades. It is superb in casseroles, stir-fries, soups, puddings, smoothies, and as a ricotta cheese substitute in dishes like lasagna or vegetable casseroles. Tofu is made from soybeans, water, and a coagulant. It is widely available in many supermarkets and health food stores. Plain tofu comes in two main forms: regular (packed in water and refrigerated) and silken (in aseptic cartons and refrigerated tubs). Each type is available in soft, firm, and extra-firm varieties. Baked tofu can be purchased in various flavors such as smoked, Italian-style, lemon pepper, and several Asian-flavored varieties. Another variety of tofu now available is sprouted tofu, which many people find easier to digest. Made from sprouted soybeans, sprouted tofu also tastes great raw.

Turmeric: Turmeric is a member of the ginger family and it is a great spice to add to your vegan recipe repertoire. Turmeric's stunning yellow/orange color adds visual beauty and its mild taste imparts depth to many savory dishes, such as recipes made with tofu, tempeh, grains, and vegetables. Turmeric provides anti-inflammatory health benefits, and it is used in both Chinese and Ayurvedic medicine. Try adding turmeric to classic rice and beans, scrambled tofu, vegan quiche, or steamed tofu with veggies.

Vegetable broth and bouillon cubes: Many brands of these handy flavor enhancers are available in most supermarkets. Keep several brands of organic vegetable broth (I like the ones packaged in aseptic cartons) in your pantry to enhance soups, stews, chilies, sauces, vegan gravies, and casseroles. Vegetable bouillon cubes are handy to use in the same manner. Try to purchase the organic cubes and make sure they are free of hydrogenated oils. Cubes are convenient to use as a last-minute flavor enhancer in many savory recipes.

Wheat germ (toasted and raw): This embryo of the wheat kernel is dense in flavor, texture, and nutrients. Wheat germ should be refrigerated after opening to prevent it from becoming rancid. Wheat germ is easily found in supermarkets and health food stores. Try the toasted variety sprinkled over pasta instead of Parmesan cheese or layered in a casserole instead of bread crumbs. It adds protein and great taste when incorporated into baked goods, casseroles, and smoothies.

Whole-grain bread, flour, and pasta: Bread, flour, and pasta made with 100 percent whole grains are considered to have a superior nutritional profile to refined grains, offering a complex, full-bodied texture and flavor. Look for the word "whole" on the package label. In addition, sprouted, flourless, and/or wheat-free whole-grain bread varieties can be readily found in many larger supermarkets. Buy certified organic bread, flour, and pasta whenever they are available to you.

Herbs and Spices

Cooking with Dried Herbs & Spices

Layers of flavor: that's the basis of great plant-based cooking. Cooking with dried herbs and spices is an easy way to jazz up your everyday recipes by adding flavorsome seasonings. I love incorporating various herbs and spices into each meal of the day, including breakfast and snacks! Simply put, adding layers of seasonings makes your food taste *delicious.*

Try to buy herbs and spices that are organic and nonirradiated whenever possible, and store them in a cool, dark place away from sunlight and heat. Check the expiration dates on your herbs and spices every six months and replace items that are past their prime. Replacing old herbs and spices with new items ensures that they will add robust aroma, appealing color, and fresh-tasting flavors to your recipes.

A word here about herb and spice seasoning blends. I have received many e-mails concerning this topic. I often use seasoning blends in my recipes because they save a lot of time in the kitchen. I believe that the easier and quicker the recipes in this book are to prepare, the more likely you are to want to re-create them in your own home kitchen. For example, when making an Italian-inspired recipe, rather than having to individually measure out marjoram, oregano, basil, rosemary, sage, and thyme (who has the time?), I suggest using an Italian seasoning blend instead. Different seasoning blends incorporate various amounts

Jazzy Tip: Consider using reusable shopping bags. Start by buying a few recyclable cloth bags. Consider also purchasing some insulated shopping bags, and you will be supporting the environment while helping your frozen and refrigerated foods to stay chilled on your trip home from the marketplace.

of herbs and even vary the herbs themselves, creating great flavors for you to add to your recipes. So by testing and purchasing numerous seasoning blends, you can cook up culinary creations in your own home kitchen that you and your family will savor while saving prep time on your meals!

Best of all, incorporating dried herbs and spices into your daily cooking allows you to create appetizing meals without adding a lot of salt, sugar, or fat to your recipes. Try creating your own jazzy seasonings by combining the herbs and spices that you and your family like best.

Here's a basic list of herbs and spices to keep regularly stocked in your spice cabinet:

HERBS AND SPICES

all-purpose seasoning (your favorite blend)	Himalayan pink salt
	Italian seasoning
allspice	marjoram
basil	nutmeg
cayenne pepper	oregano
chili powder	paprika
cilantro	parsley
cinnamon (ground)	pepper (freshly ground and coarse and
crushed red pepper	fine pre-ground black pepper)
cumin (ground)	rosemary
dill weed	sage
garlic powder	sea salt (coarse and fine ground)
ginger	turmeric

Cooking with Fresh Herbs

Cooking with fresh herbs adds flavor to your recipes, while often also adding desirable health properties. All summer long, I incorporate fresh herbs into my daily recipes.

Using fresh herbs enables you to create delicious meals without adding extra salt, sugar, or fat. Dried herbs are great, but for fabulously fresh flavor, nothing exceeds the taste of fresh herbs, which add living vitality to salads, pastas, casseroles, sandwiches, beverages, soups, and even desserts! In most recipes, you can substitute chopped, fresh herbs for dried. Because dried herbs are more concentrated than fresh herbs, increase the amount of fresh herbs; in general, use three times as much as the amount of dried herbs called for.

MY TOP 10 FAVORITE FRESH SUMMER HERBS

basil (all varieties, including genovese, lemon, Thai, cinnamon, and purple, to name a few)
chives
cilantro
oregano
parsley
peppermint
rosemary
sage (I like purple and golden)
spearmint
thyme

I particularly love cooking with fresh basil. It adds zing to so many summertime recipes. Use it instead of lettuce in sandwiches and wraps. Add it to pasta sauces, savory baked goods, chilled soups, and seasonal salads. You can make a great quick summer salad by simply cutting cherry or grape tomatoes in half, adding chopped fresh basil, chopped fresh garlic, and a bit of sea salt and pepper. Toss well and serve!

The best way to chop large-leaved fresh herbs (such as basil or sage) is to stack six to ten leaves on your cutting board, and then roll them up tightly like a cigar. You can easily cut across the cylinder of leaves, making beautiful little chiffonade strips that you can add to recipes in a jiffy.

Many herbs are hardy and easy to grow in the warmer months. During the summer months, think about growing your own fresh herbs in your yard, in containers on your deck, or even in window boxes. I grow herbs in containers placed in a sunny spot on my back deck all summer long. Some of my favorite varieties of fresh herbs to grow are basil, rosemary, spearmint, thyme, oregano, sage, and parsley. I like to grow some basic greens, too, like arugula, romaine, kale, mizuna, and tatsoi. (If you have not tried mizuna and tatsoi, they make a great addition to any garden. The baby leaves of both varieties are quite tender and add a welcome crunch to summer salads. Mizuna has pretty feather-like leaves and a peppery taste, while tatsoi has dark green, spoon-shaped leaves and a slight mustard taste. Mature mizuna and tatsoi are tasty steamed or added to nearly cooked soups.)

It's best to use fresh herbs shortly after you harvest or purchase them. If you won't be using them right away, wrap them loosely in a paper towel and store them in a spacious container or plastic bag in the vegetable compartment of your refrigerator. Don't chop them until you're ready to use them.

If you purchase a large bunch of fresh herbs that still has the roots attached, you can store it in water, just like fresh flowers. First, rinse the roots briefly, and give them a fresh cut. Then place the herbs in a vase or pitcher of water and keep them on your kitchen counter. That way you can easily pinch off a few leaves as you are cooking.

You can create your own signature flavor blend by combining summer herbs that you prefer. It's the easiest way to jazz up your warm-weather recipes, resulting in delicious, personalized creations that you, your friends, and your family will savor. Give it a try!

Helpful Tips for Low-Fat Cooking

I receive a lot of e-mail inquiries asking how to lower or eliminate fat from recipes while keeping them flavorful and delicious. It is really much easier to do than you may think! Here are a just few of my favorite "go-to" solutions for creating lower-fat dishes in your own home kitchen.

In savory dishes, replace all of the oil used in the recipe with low-fat, unsalted vegetable broth or water. Use three tablespoons of either broth or water to replace one tablespoon of oil. Unlike oil, broth or water will evaporate quickly during cooking, so keep an eye out and add more liquid, about two tablespoons at a time as needed, if your pan becomes dry.

—— FAT VS. BROTH ——

1 tablespoon oil = 3 tablespoons of low-fat vegetable broth or water

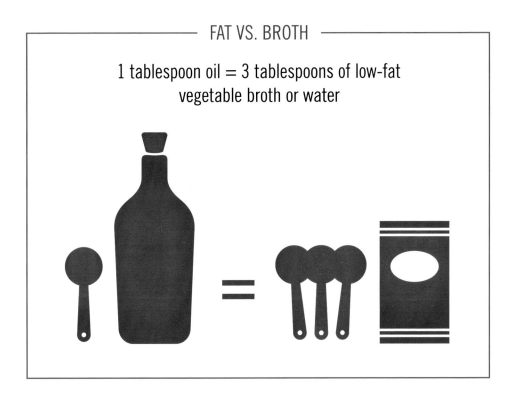

In baked goods recipes like muffins or cakes, use fresh apple purée to replace all of the oil and some of the sugar. This is a great way to add fruit into your family's diet while cutting down on fat and sugar. Simply peel and core apples, and then purée them in a blender until they have the consistency of a smooth applesauce. Start by adding the apple purée in the same ratio you would add oil to the recipe. When using the apple purée, you may have to add more liquid to your recipe. If the batter seems too dry after adding the apple purée, add more nondairy milk, one tablespoon at a time, until the desired consistency is achieved. In addition, cut down on the sugar in the recipe by 25 percent.

In general, substituting *flavor* for *oil* will make your plant-based recipes low in fat and high in great taste. Now that is jazzy!

Tips for Improvisation

The recipes in this book can be personalized for your particular needs. If you have food allergies or sensitivities, feel free to improvise, just like the jazz greats do with a piece of music!

If you are wondering why I do not always list exact amounts for salt and pepper in some of the recipes, here is my reasoning. If a recipe needs a precise amount of salt or pepper to make it taste optimal, I have listed the amount in the ingredients list, but if the addition of salt and pepper to a recipe is optional, I have left the salt and pepper amounts to you, in order to personalize the dishes to your own specific tastes.

To guide readers who are following a nut-free and/or oil-free diet, I have added [NUT FREE] and [OIL FREE] throughout the book to recipes that are void of nuts or oil. In addition, I have added comments for gluten-free cooking and baking options in the notes of many recipes. I hope this will be helpful for those whose diets are restricted.

Table of Equivalent Measures

I have probably measured ingredients in my recipes thousands of times, but I still never seem to remember the table of equivalent measures. My good friend Suzanne is a gourmet cook, and one day she told me that one of her favorite "extra" features in my books was the table of measures! So I thought I'd include it here for convenient reference. This table is handy to refer to when doubling or tripling recipes, cooking up new recipes, or cutting an existing recipe in half. I know you'll find it as helpful as I do!

This — IS THE SAME AS →	*This*
3 teaspoons	1 tablespoon
4 tablespoons	¼ cup
8 tablespoons	½ cup
12 tablespoons	¾ cup
16 tablespoons	1 cup (or 8 ounces)
2 cups	1 pint (or 16 ounces)
4 cups	1 quart (or 32 ounces)
4 quarts	1 gallon (or 128 ounces)

Chilled Avocado Soup
(page 109)

Cashew and Quinoa Loaf
(page 166)

Asparagus with Vegan
Hollandaise Sauce
(page 201)

Chocolate Ganache Cake
(page 238)

Chapter 2

Menus Made Easy

I believe that a well-planned menu makes for a perfect meal. Sometimes the most demanding part of hosting a dinner party or serving a family meal is deciding what foods to pair together. Even after 20 years of hosting vegan parties, family get-togethers, and simple weeknight meals, I still feel challenged when figuring out my menu plan!

"*Whatever she does to my songs, she always makes them sound better.*"

——Songwriter Richard Rodgers on Ella Fitzgerald

Here I have made meal planning easy by providing delicious and diverse full menu plans for any occasion. These 10 menus include my jazzy recipes for serving American classic family meals—all with a vegan twist. From four-course to no-course, breakfast to brunch, and holiday fare to weekday dining, these jazzylicious menus featuring recipes included in this book can help you to create luscious plant-based meals that will please you, your family, and friends.

On another note, I love to listen to beautiful music while dining and I think you may, too. The right music choice helps to set the mood for any gala or get-together. As a recording artist, singer, actor, television personality, radio host, and producer, I have had the privilege to work with, interview, and feature the music of countless gifted musical performers on my radio show. Because of this, I have enhanced each menu plan with my recommended Jazzy Music Pick. Whether you are looking for music to dine, cook, or relax to, I hope you find these musical selections as enchanting as I do.

Bon appétit!

Good Morning Fiesta

Is breakfast getting a little humdrum at your house? Looking to liven up your morning meals? Switching up run-of-the-mill a.m. fare for appealing new dishes can be challenging, but this exciting menu features festive recipes that are sure to wake up your good-morning meal. So let's have a morning fiesta!

main dish
Tofu Ranchero
(page 81)

side dish
Magnificent Maple Granola with
Banana Whipped Topping
(page 79)

baked goods
Cornbread and Sweet Pepper Mini-Muffins
(page 96)

beverage
Pineapple-Banana-Strawberry Smoothie
(page 86)

Jazzy Music Pick

Johannes Linstead, *Mistico*

In addition to being a guitar star, Johannes Linstead is a vegan, yoga master, and author of the self-help book Buddha in a Business Suit. Mistico *explores the many nuances of the Spanish guitar, from the traditional to the contemporary, from the passionate to the fiery. Exotic sounds weave together with exciting rhythms to create an album that enriches this breakfast fiesta menu.*

{ MENU 2 }

Lunch Bunch

I love hosting a fabulous midday meal for my girlfriends. I like focusing on simple fare like the dishes featured in this menu. Begin the meal with an easily prepared soup followed by refreshing salads. I like to serve a duo or trio of main-dish salads on a bed of Boston lettuce. (These salads can fly solo, too, so mix or match as you please!) A refreshing and elegant simple sorbet rounds out this appealing lineup. Let's get ready for the lunch bunch!

soup
Four-Ingredient Leek Soup
(page 105)

main dishes
Penne and Black Bean Salad
(page 137)

Fancy Chickpea Salad
(page 127)

Quinoa Tabbouleh
(page 140)

dessert
Banana-Raspberry Sorbet
(page 272)

beverage
Very-Berry Summer Tea
(page 73)

Jazzy Music Pick

Oscar Peterson and Stéphane Grappelli, *Jazz in Paris: Oscar Peterson–Stéphane Grappelli Quartet, Vol. 1*

Experience the genius of two of the greatest jazz artists in piano and violin with this cheerful album. The two legendary artists that comprise this alluring musical duo complement each other beautifully in these mesmerizing tunes, many of them fun and upbeat. Grappelli's soaring violin amplifies Peterson's classic jazz piano style in a way that surely will transport your lunch bunch party to a chic Parisian café.

Portable Picnic

Summertime is the time to share a fun and festive outdoor picnic with the kids, family, or friends. This menu begins with an asparagus salad that gives zing to this portable menu. Pair it with an exciting main-dish salad served in edible bowls. For dessert, festive lollipops add fun and flavor, and homemade lemonade rounds out this perfect picnic with frosty freshness.

salad
Marinated Asparagus Salad
(page 136)

main dish
Chickpea and Quinoa Salad in Sweet Pepper Boats
(page 143)

baked goods
Cinnamon-Maple Mini-Muffins
(page 98)

dessert
Chocolate Date-Nut Lollipops
(page 250)

beverage
Beautiful Basil Lemonade
(page 73)

Jazzy Music Pick

Terry Blaine, *Whose Honey Are You?*

On her acclaimed debut album, Ms. Blaine shines as a bright singing star on the American musical horizon. Forging a fresh link in the regal chain that recalls the tradition of Billie Holiday, Bessie Smith, Ethel Waters, and others, Terry's style of singing is a gentle, swinging reminder of who we were and where we came from. This upbeat collection of 14 classic jazz gems has a feel-good quality that makes excellent accompaniment for any festal, fabulous, and fun picnic meal.

BBQ Bash

It's barbecue time! The fresh tastes of summer are beautifully showcased in this easy, breezy, and delicious menu. Whether you are grilling outdoors or cooking up a barbecue-style meal in your kitchen, this menu evokes the flavors of classic grilling recipes. I like to build the bill of fare for a summer barbecue around foods found at my local farmers' market. This summer your barbecue can be healthy and easy to prepare, but best of all, it can be jazzylicious!

soup
Chilled Avocado Soup
(page 109)

salad
Kale and Tomato Salad
(page 129)

main dish
Jazzylicious Shish Kebabs
(page 176)

side dish
Quick Quinoa
(page 219)

dessert
Choco-Peanut Butter Cups
(page 249)

Jazzy Music Pick

Lance Horne,
First Things Last

Vegetarian Lance Horne creates a fanciful feeling on his debut album, making an entertaining collection for any outdoor summertime meal. Mr. Horne is a well-known composer, lyricist, singer, pianist, and music director, and here he connects familiar sounds from musical theater and beyond. This compilation highlights his talent on piano along with an array of special guest vocalists that include Alan Cumming, Amanda Palmer, Cheyenne Jackson, and Ricki Lake.

All-American Burger and Fries

What's the quintessential American meal? A burger and fries. Sometimes I get a craving for this American classic—one of my favorite childhood meals—so I've created a fabulous vegan version. This menu features my healthy and tasty twist on the traditional burger and fries served up with coleslaw and a dairy-free milk shake. For a sweet finish, classic chocolate chip cookies are sure to please.

main dish
Mushroom-Nut Burgers
(page 185)

side dish
Confetti Oven Fries
(page 217)

Pretty Purple Coleslaw
(page 130)

desserts
Banana Milk-less Shake
(page 255)

Chewy Chocolate Chip Cookies
(page 226)

Jazzy Music Pick

**Jerry Ragovoy, *The Jerry Ragovoy
Story: Time is on My Side 1953–2003***

*This invigorating release puts the spotlight on my late great
friend, superstar songwriter-arranger-producer Jerry
Ragovoy. Ragovoy's production work and songwriting skills
exemplify the classic New York "Big City" sound of the 1960s,
and this album highlights 24 of his brilliant recordings.
The CD booklet contains a 2008 interview with Ragovoy,
specially conducted for the project by another songwriting
legend, Al Kooper. This all-American classic recording pairs
pleasingly with this fun burger-and-fries-style meal.*

Wheatloaf and Potatoes Dinner

Here is a classic meal that's great to serve for a festive weekend supper or fancy dinner with friends. This menu features a meaty-tasting main dish loaf served with savory gravy. On the side, serve my version of Grandma's fabulous potatoes and broccoli with a sweet sauce. For dessert, offer a luscious and creamy pie.

salad
Spinach and Apple Salad with Maple-Mustard Dressing
(page 124)

main dish
Savory Seitan Loaf
with Tomato-Mushroom Gravy
(page 192)

side dishes
Twice-Baked Potatoes
(page 214)

Broccoli with Sweet Tamari-Onion Sauce
(page 204)

dessert
Dreamy Banana Pie
(page 263)

Jazzy Music Pick

Michael Feinstein, *The Sinatra Project, Vol II: The Good Life*

This elegant album provides an ideal mix of Sinatra classics to enhance any festive menu. Michael Feinstein, the multiplatinum-selling, five-time Grammy-nominated entertainer dubbed "the Ambassador of the Great American Songbook," is considered one of the premier interpreters of American standards—and he's a vegan! The captivating tunes on this album pair seamlessly with this hearty family meal.

A Taste of Italy

What's more Italian-American than spaghetti and meatballs? This menu features my delicious vegan version of this much-loved staple. With a simple salad and sweet dessert to round out the menu you can serve this hearty meal with confidence. A family menu is never dull when the star of the meal is pasta!

salad
Caesar Salad, Jazzy-Style
(page 120)

with

Cashew Parmesan
(page 57)

main dish
Spaghetti and Wheatballs
(page 150)

with

Dad's Marinara
(page 48)

side dish
Broccoli with Lemon Sauce
(page 202)

dessert
Pear, Apple, and Walnut Crostata
(page 264)

Jazzy Music Pick

Michéal Castaldo, *Olive You (Classic Italian Songs to Feed the Heart & Soul)*

Popular classical crooner Michéal Castaldo shines on this stunning album. Evoking the imagery of the sunbathed Italian landscape, the album is the perfect vehicle for Castaldo's pièce de résistance—his voice. The uplifting tunes in this collection are the perfect recipe of sound and melodic timbre that pair well with this Italian-inspired menu.

{ MENU 8 }

Festive Family Meal

A celebratory family get-together calls for an appealing menu filled with traditional tastes. This menu shares some of my favorites served up with a jazzy twist. Stuffed cabbage, based on my mother-in-law's delicious recipe, is the satisfying superstar of this meal, served with a side of creamy mashed potatoes. For the first course, traditionally inspired charoset adds color and crunch to this festal meal. To finish with a flourish, coconut cookies make the perfect sweet treat.

salad

Apple, Walnut, and Cinnamon Salad (Anita's Charoset)

(page 130)

main dish

Sweet and Sour Stuffed Cabbage

(page 186)

side dishes

Mashed Potatoes with Roasted Garlic

(page 218)

Steamed Green Beans and Carrots with Orange Sauce

(page 207)

dessert

Coconut Vegaroons

(page 233)

Jazzy Music Pick

Paul Winter Sextet, *Count Me In* (*50th Anniversary Anthology*)

This festive 50th anniversary anthology includes tracks from the Sextet's historic concert at the Kennedy White House. This recording is both exuberant and warm, as the two-volume CD soars through an incredibly balanced group of tunes, finding flawless harmony between the improvised and the composed. A lovely accompaniment to this gala family menu!

Giving Thanks

Holiday parties can be challenging when you are trying to serve a merry meal for vegans, vegetarians, and omnivores alike. But fret no more. This jazzylicious Thanksgiving menu will please all diners at your soirée. The main course features a scrumptious savory stuffing casserole paired with sweet winter squash. Delectable, homemade pumpkin pie served up with a twist finishes this meal on a jazzy but classic note.

soup
Best Butternut Bisque
(page 112)

salad
Festive Kale Salad
(page 126)

main dish
Holiday White Bean, Potato, and Stuffing Casserole
(page 194)

side dishes
Maple-Baked Acorn Squash
(page 208)

Petite Peas and Parsnips
(page 202)

dessert
Pumpkin Pie with Date-Nut Crust
(page 260)

Jazzy Music Pick

Laura Theodore,
What The World Needs Now Is Love

It's time for me to share the "jazz" in the Jazzy Vegetarian with one of my signature recordings. Festive and upbeat, this album features many of my favorite popular standards along with a few lesser-known gems. Featuring several arrangements and solos from the late, great "Saxy Lady" Juliene Purefoy and her big band, this musical collection will beautifully enhance your giving thanks meal.

Winter Celebration

When snowflakes begin to fall, and winter's white blanket settles in, it's time to get cozy with family and friends by serving this warming menu. My stepmom always serves tempting Italian favorites during the winter holidays, while my dad is in charge of making his delicious sauce. Following their example, here is my delightful Italian-American-inspired menu fit for any cold-weather celebration!

soup
Butternut Squash and White Bean Soup
(page 110)

salad
Quick Baby Spinach Salad
(page 123)

main dish
Festive Stuffed Shells with Dad's Marinara
(page 148)   *and*   *(page 48)*

side dish
Green Beans Almondine
(page 205)

dessert
Black Forest Pecan Pie with Vanilla "Crème Fresh"
(page 258)   *and*   *(page 60)*

Holiday Sandies Cookies
(page 235)

Jazzy Music Pick

Jim Brickman,
All Is Calm: Peaceful Christmas Hymns

A brilliant assortment of holiday-inspired tunes by popular songwriter and piano man Jim Brickman creates a peaceful mood for this seasonal-soirée menu. This awesome musical celebration—a beautiful collection of calming Christmas hymns—focuses on Brickman's hypnotizing piano style, and is highlighted by the magical and memorable "Fa La La," featuring Genevieve Bellemare. It's the ideal musical centerpiece for any festive winter celebration.

Cashew and Quinoa Loaf
(page 166)
Asparagus with Vegan
Hollandaise Sauce
(page 201)

Chapter 3

Sauces, Dressings, and Accompaniments

Let's get saucy! There's nothing like a flavorful sauce to dress up your meal. I love adding a yummy sauce or dressing to easy-to-prepare, classic foods like pastas, salads, casseroles, and steamed veggies in order to wake up their hidden taste. And nothing makes a dessert jazzier than a scrumptious, creamy-*tasting*, whipped topping. Try pairing the delectable toppings included in this chapter with your own plant-based creations and they'll be incredibly delicious. Oh yes, please be ready: your family and friends may ask for seconds!

"One thing I like about jazz, kid, is that I don't know what's going to happen next. Do you?"

——Bix Beiderbecke

Quick Barbecue Sauce

[MAKES 4 SERVINGS] [NUT FREE, NO OIL] Sometimes the taste of a freshly made barbecue sauce is what you need to add extra pizzazz to shish kebabs, nut burgers, or casseroles.

⅓ cup catsup
¼ cup diced onion
2 tablespoons unsulphured blackstrap
   molasses, plus more as needed
1 heaping teaspoon brown sugar
½ teaspoon chili powder
½ teaspoon garlic powder
⅛ to ¼ teaspoon cayenne pepper

Put all of the ingredients in a small bowl and whisk to combine. If the mixture seems too thin, add more molasses, 1 tablespoon at a time (up to 4 tablespoons in all), to achieve the desired consistency.

Zesty BBQ Sauce

[MAKES 5 TO 6 SERVINGS] [NUT FREE, NO OIL] This recipe offers the perfect solution if you don't want to resort to using a bottled variety. Pour a little of this, shake a little of that, and presto . . . you have a delish sauce to enhance any grilled delight!

1 cup catsup
⅓ cup unsulphured blackstrap
   molasses
2 heaping teaspoons brown sugar or
   maple sugar
1 teaspoon balsamic vinegar
1 teaspoon tamari
1 teaspoon chili powder
¼ teaspoon garlic powder
1/16 to ⅛ teaspoon cayenne pepper

Put all of the ingredients in a small bowl and whisk to combine.

Maple-Scallion Dipping Sauce

Tomato-Mushroom Gravy

[MAKES 6 SERVINGS] [NUT FREE] My stepmom, who is an excellent cook, taught me an authentic Italian method of using tomato paste that adds great taste to any basic soup stock. I took it a step further here and used her technique to flavor this fabulous, easy-to-prepare gravy that pairs beautifully with so many dishes.

¼ cup tomato paste
1 teaspoon extra-virgin olive oil
1½ cups filtered or spring water,
    plus more as needed
1 clove garlic, minced
2½ cups sliced cremini or white
    button mushrooms
1 teaspoon Italian seasoning
½ teaspoon reduced-sodium tamari

Put the tomato paste, olive oil, 3 tablespoons water, and garlic in a large skillet. Cook over medium heat for 2 minutes, stirring constantly. If the mixture starts to stick to the bottom of the skillet, add more water, 1 tablespoon at a time. Decrease the heat to medium-low. Add 1 cup water, the mushrooms, Italian seasoning, and tamari. Cover and cook for 15 to 20 minutes, until the mushrooms are soft. Add more water, ¼ cup at a time, if needed, to thin the gravy to the desired consistency.

Maple-Scallion Dipping Sauce

[MAKES 3 SERVINGS] [NUT FREE, NO OIL] This sweet and rich sauce imparts a bit of an Asian flair that is perfect to pair with tofu, tempeh, or even steamed veggies. The best part is that it uses only three ingredients, but the taste is full-bodied, delicate, and rich.

3 tablespoons maple syrup
1 tablespoon regular or reduced-
    sodium tamari
1 small scallion, thinly sliced

Put the maple syrup and tamari in a small bowl. Whisk to combine. Divide equally into 3 dipping bowls. Top each serving with some of the sliced scallion.

Basic Tahini Sauce

[MAKES 4 SERVINGS] A good basic recipe for tahini sauce is a must for flavoring salads, casseroles, sandwiches, and vegetables. Here is my quick-to-prepare, go-to version of this traditional vegan sauce.

2 tablespoons sesame tahini, plus more as needed
1 large clove garlic, minced
1 teaspoon regular or reduced-sodium tamari
⅛ teaspoon cayenne pepper
¼ cup filtered or spring water, plus more as needed

Put all of the ingredients in a small mixing bowl. Whisk until smooth and creamy. If the sauce seems too thin, add more tahini, 1 teaspoon at a time. If the sauce seems too thick, add more water, 1 teaspoon at a time.

Lemon Tahini Sauce

[MAKES 4 TO 6 SERVINGS] The zesty pop of lemon in this sauce combines beautifully with the mellow taste of the tahini, making an ideal topping for a crisp green salad, cruciferous veggies like broccoli and cauliflower, or steamed greens like kale, spinach, or Swiss chard.

3 tablespoons sesame tahini, plus more as needed
1 tablespoon freshly squeezed lemon juice
1 clove garlic, minced
⅛ teaspoon cayenne pepper
4 tablespoons filtered or spring water, plus more as needed

Put all of the ingredients in a small mixing bowl. Whisk until smooth and creamy. If the sauce seems too thin, add more tahini, 1 teaspoon at a time. If the sauce seems too thick, add more water, 1 teaspoon at a time.

Peanut Sauce

[MAKES 2 TO 4 SERVINGS] This creamy sauce makes a wonderful addition to cooked soba noodles, whole-wheat linguini, gluten-free pasta, or even plain old spaghetti. It is tasty, too, served over steamed fresh vegetables or greens.

---

3 tablespoons filtered or spring
　　water, plus more as needed
2 tablespoons peanut butter
　　(creamy or chunky)
2 cloves garlic, minced
¼ teaspoon sea salt
¼ teaspoon chili powder
⅛ teaspoon cayenne pepper

Put all of the ingredients in a medium bowl. Whisk briskly until smooth.

Vegan Hollandaise Sauce

[MAKES 4 TO 5 SERVINGS] [NUT FREE, NO OIL] Several years ago my dad asked me to come up with a low-fat hollandaise-style sauce, so I put on my jazzy thinking cap and created this delicious and easy version. With only four ingredients, this delicate sauce has a surprisingly rich taste and makes the perfect topper for asparagus or for any dish requiring a hollandaise sauce!

---

8 ounces soft silken or regular tofu,
　　drained
3 tablespoons freshly squeezed
　　lemon juice
¼ teaspoon turmeric
¼ teaspoon sea salt

Put all of the ingredients in a blender and process until smooth and creamy. Pour into a small sauce pan and cook over low heat, stirring constantly, until heated through. Serve immediately.

Dad's Marinara

[MAKES 4 TO 6 SERVINGS] [NUT FREE, NO OIL] My dad makes a fabulous marinara that is always a top request at any family gathering. The longer you cook it, the more complex the sauce becomes. Use it to top plain spaghetti or any other kind of pasta, or use it as a base for lasagna, stuffed shells, or casseroles.

---

1 can (28 ounces) crushed tomatoes (I use crushed tomatoes, but Dad uses canned tomato *sauce*)

1 cup filtered or spring water, plus more as needed

3 cloves garlic, minced, or ½ teaspoon garlic powder

1½ teaspoons dried basil

1 teaspoon dried oregano

½ teaspoon dried parsley

¼ teaspoon crushed red pepper (⅛ teaspoon for a less spicy sauce)

2 tablespoons good red wine (optional)

Sea salt or Himalayan pink salt, to taste

Put the tomatoes, water, garlic, basil, oregano, parsley, and crushed red pepper in a large sauce pan. If mixture seems too thick, add ¼ cup water. Stir to combine. Bring to a simmer over medium heat.

Decrease the heat to medium-low, cover, and simmer, stirring occasionally, for 45 minutes. If desired, add the optional red wine at this point.

Simmer for 15 to 30 minutes more, or up to 2 hours (the longer you cook it, the more developed the flavors will be). Add salt to taste, if desired. Serve over whole-grain pasta of your choice.

Tasty Teriyaki Sauce

[MAKES 2 SERVINGS] [NUT FREE, NO OIL] Teriyaki sauce makes a great marinade for tofu, tempeh, seitan, portobello mushrooms, and much more. This simple-to-prepare version employs maple syrup to add thickness and taste. For a denser and sweeter sauce, just add more maple syrup to taste.

1 tablespoon reduced-sodium
   tamari
1 teaspoon maple syrup
1 clove garlic, minced

Put all of the ingredients in a small bowl and whisk until smooth.

Sweet Tamari-Onion Sauce

[MAKES 2 TO 4 SERVINGS] [NUT FREE, NO OIL] I love this sauce mixed with freshly steamed vegetables of any kind. Simply steam your favorites and toss with the sauce while they are piping hot, and you have perfectly flavored veggies!

1 tablespoon regular or reduced-
   sodium tamari
1 tablespoon maple sugar
1 tablespoon minced sweet onion
1 large clove garlic, minced

Put all of the ingredients in a small bowl and whisk to combine.

Four-Ingredient Dijon Dressing

[MAKES 2 SERVINGS] [NUT FREE, NO OIL] My husband loves a sweet Dijon-style dressing, so I came up with this four-ingredient version that whips up quickly and tastes like the real deal.

1 tablespoon Dijon mustard
1 tablespoon maple syrup
1 teaspoon balsamic vinegar
1 clove garlic, minced

Put all of the ingredients in a small bowl and whisk together until smooth.

Maple-Mustard Dressing

[MAKES 4 TO 6 SERVINGS] [NUT FREE, NO OIL] My slightly altered version of this salad staple uses a dash of cayenne pepper to spice things up a bit.

4 heaping tablespoons Dijon
    mustard
2 tablespoons maple syrup
2 cloves garlic, minced
1 tablespoon filtered or spring
    water, plus more as needed
¼ teaspoon sea salt
Pinch of cayenne pepper

Put all of the ingredients in a small mixing bowl. Whisk until smooth. Add more water, if needed, 1 teaspoon at a time, to achieve the desired consistency.

For a sweeter dressing, just add a bit more maple syrup.

Caesar Salad Dressing

[MAKES 4 TO 6 SERVINGS] [NUT FREE, NO OIL] For years I yearned for a delicious vegan version of this classic dressing, and I was really jazzed when I came up with this delightful mix of easy ingredients. The capers stand in beautifully for anchovies and the tofu replaces the egg with ease. Deeeeee-lish!

---

8 ounces firm regular tofu, drained
2 tablespoons freshly squeezed
    lemon juice
2 teaspoons capers, drained and
    rinsed
1 heaping teaspoon Dijon mustard
1 medium clove garlic
⅛ teaspoon sea salt
Freshly ground pepper, to taste

Put the tofu, lemon juice, capers, Dijon, garlic, and salt in a blender and process until smooth and creamy. If the mixture seems too thick, add a bit of filtered or spring water, 1 tablespoon at a time, to achieve the desired consistency. Add freshly ground pepper to taste.

Simple Lemon and Maple Dressing

[MAKES 2 SERVINGS] [NUT FREE, NO OIL] I would never have thought that two simple and basic ingredients could make such a delish dressing, but this combination tastes fabulous! This is my go-to topping for a crisp green salad or for dressing up thinly sliced raw kale.

---

1 tablespoon freshly squeezed
    lemon juice
1 tablespoon maple syrup

Put the lemon juice and maple syrup in a small bowl and whisk briskly until smooth.

Lively Lemon Salad Dressing

[MAKES 4 SERVINGS] [NUT FREE] This is a gorgeous dressing to give extra punch to green and grain-based salads. It is particularly appetizing in the summer months because the pop of lemon imparts a fresh zing.

---

4 tablespoons freshly squeezed
    lemon juice
3 teaspoons extra-virgin olive oil
1 teaspoon maple syrup
1 large clove garlic, minced
Sea salt, to taste
Freshly ground pepper, to taste

Put the lemon juice, olive oil, maple syrup, and garlic in a small bowl and whisk briskly until smooth and emulsified. Season with salt and pepper to taste.

Orange-Tahini Dressing

[MAKES 4 TO 6 SERVINGS] The sweet and subtly acidic flavor of oranges complements the earthy sesame seed notes of the tahini in this creamy, smooth, and slightly sweet dressing—perfect for tossing with romaine lettuce for a quick dinner salad or, for a different tasty treat, as a topping for fresh fruit.

---

4 tablespoons freshly squeezed
    or refrigerated store-bought
    orange juice
1 clove garlic, minced
2 tablespoons maple syrup
2 heaping tablespoons sesame tahini
1 teaspoon balsamic vinegar

Put all of the ingredients in small bowl and whisk until smooth. If the dressing is too thick, add filtered or spring water, 1 tablespoon at a time, to achieve the desired consistency.

Very Balsamic Salad Dressing

[MAKES 4 SERVINGS] [NUT FREE] This basic balsamic dressing will give your salad real zing. This adaptation boasts a rich balsamic taste with just a touch of sweet.

2 tablespoons extra-virgin olive oil
2 tablespoons balsamic vinegar
1 to 2 teaspoons brown sugar or
    maple sugar
1 teaspoon Dijon mustard
Sea salt, to taste (optional)
Freshly ground pepper, to taste
    (optional)

Put the olive oil, vinegar, sugar, and Dijon in a small bowl and whisk briskly until smooth and emulsified. Season with salt and pepper, if desired.

Creamy Dijon–Mayonnaise Dressing

[MAKES 6 SERVINGS] [NUT FREE] This is a wonderful dressing to serve when entertaining guests because it mimics the taste of the store-bought, non-vegan bottled varieties without sacrificing good taste. It can be made well in advance of serving, which is a plus for time-crunched meal prep!

⅓ cup vegan mayonnaise (see note)
¼ cup Dijon mustard
1 heaping tablespoon brown sugar
    or maple sugar
1 teaspoon Italian or all-purpose
    seasoning
Sea salt, to taste
Freshly ground pepper, to taste

Put the vegan mayonnaise, Dijon, sugar, and Italian or all-purpose seasoning in a small bowl and whisk until smooth. Add salt and pepper to taste.

—— CHEF'S NOTE ——

Plain vegan yogurt may be substituted for the vegan mayonnaise in this recipe.

Vegan Sour "Cream"

[MAKES 6 TO 8 SERVINGS] [NUT FREE, NO OIL] This realistic substitute for the dairy variety works well as a base for dressings and dips, spooned over baked potatoes or chili, or served with my Easy Burrito Bake (page 169). When I served this to the crew on the set of my television show, they were amazed by how much it tastes like actual sour cream!

---

14 to 16 ounces soft or firm silken tofu, drained (sprouted variety is preferable; see note)
1½ to 2 tablespoons freshly squeezed lemon juice
⅛ to ¼ teaspoon sea salt

Put the tofu, 1½ tablespoons lemon juice, and ⅛ teaspoon sea salt in a blender and process until smooth. Taste and add additional lemon juice and sea salt, if desired. Refrigerate 1 hour and serve.

CHEF'S NOTE

This recipe will work with either soft or firm silken tofu, but the product you use will determine the consistency of your sour "cream." A soft tofu will create a looser consistency, while the firm variety will produce a firmer result.

Cashew Parmesan (opposite)
Spaghetti and Wheatballs (page 150)

Cashew Parmesan

[MAKES 15 SERVINGS] This cheese-less Parmesan imparts a creamy taste and realistic texture.

½ cup raw cashews
¼ teaspoon sea salt or Himalayan pink salt, plus more as needed

Put the cashews and salt in a blender and process until the consistency of crumbled Parmesan cheese is achieved. Don't overprocess. Taste and add more salt, if desired. Store tightly covered in the refrigerator for up to 2 days.

VARIATION

Cashew Lemon Parmesan:
Add 1 teaspoon of lemon zest. Proceed as directed.

Almond Parmesan

[MAKES 15 SERVINGS] Almonds, walnuts, or pumpkin seeds deliver slightly varied tastes and textures to this faux cheese alternative.

½ cup raw almonds
¼ teaspoon sea salt or Himalayan pink salt, plus more as needed

Put the almonds and salt in a blender and process until the consistency of crumbled Parmesan cheese is achieved. Taste and add more salt, if desired.

VARIATION

Walnut Parmesan:
Substitute walnuts for the almonds. Proceed as directed.

VARIATION

Pumpkin Seed Parmesan: Substitute pumpkin seeds for the almonds. Proceed as directed.

Banana Whipped Topping

[MAKES 4 SERVINGS] [NUT FREE, NO OIL] This wonderfully creamy whipped topping tastes great on granola, spooned over fresh fruit, or even served by itself for a light dessert!

8 ounces soft or firm regular tofu, drained (sprouted variety is preferred)
1 ripe banana
2 tablespoons maple syrup, plus more as needed

Put all of the ingredients in a blender and process until very smooth. Taste and add more maple syrup if a sweeter flavor is desired.

Bourbon Vanilla Whipped "Cream"

[MAKES 6 TO 8 SERVINGS] [NUT FREE, NO OIL] This delicious sweet topping stands in for dairy whipped cream in any recipe in need of that classic creamy taste. In addition, it is dense enough that it can be piped onto cakes and pies in a decorative fashion, much like how I have used it on top of my holiday Pumpkin Pie with Date-Nut Crust (page 260). Pure vanilla extract made with bourbon adds a bit of spark to this topping.

14 to 16 ounces extra-firm regular tofu, drained (sprouted variety is preferable)
3 tablespoons maple syrup, plus more as needed
1 teaspoon bourbon-flavored or plain vanilla extract

Put all of the ingredients in a blender and process until smooth. Taste and add more maple syrup if a sweeter flavor is desired. Refrigerate 2 to 4 hours and serve.

Bourbon Vanilla Whipped "Cream"

Vanilla "Crème Fresh"

[MAKES 4 SERVINGS] [NUT FREE, NO OIL] This fabulous faux version of classic crème fraîche is slightly sweet and totally delicious served over cakes, pies, fresh fruit, or tarts. Your family and guests are gonna love it!

8 ounces extra-firm regular tofu, drained (sprouted variety is preferable)

2 tablespoons maple syrup, plus more as needed

1 tablespoon nondairy milk, plus more as needed

1 teaspoon vanilla extract

Put all of the ingredients in a blender and process until smooth. Taste and add more maple syrup if you prefer a sweeter flavor. If the sauce is too thick, add more nondairy milk, a teaspoon at a time, until the desired consistency is reached. Refrigerate 2 to 4 hours and serve.

Mom's Pumpkin Pie Spice

[MAKES ¼ CUP] [NUT FREE, NO OIL] This spice combination is one of my mom's recipes. It showcases the perfect blend of flavors to enhance any pumpkin pie, cookie, or cake that calls for this classic sweet-and-spicy taste. It's great in oatmeal, too! Feel free to add or subtract spices that you prefer in order to create a personalized combination.

1 tablespoon ground cinnamon
1 tablespoon ground ginger
1 tablespoon ground nutmeg
1 tablespoon ground allspice

Put all of the ingredients in a small bowl and stir with a dry whisk to combine. Store in a tightly sealed container in a dry place away from sunlight.

Vanilla "Crème Fresh"

Party Potato Skins (page 71)

Chapter 4

Nibbles, Noshes, and Thirst Quenchers

Sometimes you need *just a little something* to snack on. A nibble. A nosh. I adore an in-between-meals quick bite, so I am excited to share my quick, easy, and delightful recipes with you. Delectable dips, appealing appetizers, savory snacks, and refreshing drinks all come together here to provide you with a refreshing break any time during the day. So, let's take a break. It's time for a snack!

"There are notes
between notes, you know."

—Sarah Vaughan

White Bean Cashew Dip

[MAKES 6 TO 8 SERVINGS] This is the dip to serve when you are looking to impress non-vegans. The cashews add richness, while the beans impart a creamy, smooth texture. A pop of freshly squeezed lemon juice and a hint of cayenne pepper round out the flavor in this wonderful recipe.

---

1 can (15 ounces) white beans, drained and rinsed
½ cup raw cashews
2 tablespoons filtered or spring water
4 teaspoons freshly squeezed lemon juice
1 clove garlic
½ teaspoon sea salt
¼ teaspoon cayenne pepper
2 tablespoons sweet red or orange pepper, diced
Dill weed or fresh dill sprigs, for garnish (optional)

Put the white beans, cashews, water, lemon juice, garlic, salt, and cayenne pepper in a high-performance blending appliance and process until smooth and creamy. Do not overprocess. Transfer to a pretty bowl and fold in the diced pepper. Top with dill (if using).

CHEF'S NOTE

Serve with carrot sticks, celery sticks, or whole-grain crackers.

Jazzy Tip: Need a quick snack on the go? Toss a piece of fresh, organic fruit such as an apple, banana, orange, or pear into your day bag to eat anytime!

Guacamole Salsa Dip

[MAKES 4 TO 6 SERVINGS] [NUT FREE] Let's salsa! Spicy, piquant, and zesty, this easy-to-prep dip will become a staple in your home kitchen.

1 cup prepared salsa
2 large avocados
1 large clove garlic, minced
½ to 1 tablespoon freshly squeezed
   lemon juice
½ tablespoon chopped fresh
   cilantro or flat-leaf parsley
⅛ teaspoon sea salt
Chopped fresh cilantro or flat-leaf
   parsley, for garnish (optional)

Put the salsa, avocados, garlic, lemon juice, cilantro or parsley, and salt in a medium-size bowl. Mash with a potato masher or large fork until combined. Place in a pretty serving bowl and garnish with chopped cilantro or parsley (if using).

Sweet and Salty Snack Almonds

[MAKES 10 TO 12 SERVINGS] My friend Sara loves these almonds. She often says this snack is one of her favorite jazzy treats! Make 'em for your friends and family, and watch big smiles magically appear.

4 cups raw almonds
3 tablespoons maple sugar
3 teaspoons reduced-sodium tamari

Preheat the oven to 400 degrees F. Put the almonds in a single layer on an 11 x 17 inch rimmed baking pan lined with unbleached parchment paper, and bake for 5 to 7 minutes or until the almonds are a light golden color. Check the almonds frequently to prevent them from over browning. Pour the almonds into a large bowl, add the maple sugar, and toss to coat. Drizzle the tamari over the almonds and continue tossing until evenly coated. Let the almonds cool at least 30 minutes before serving.

Spicy Dip

[MAKES 4 SERVINGS] [NUT FREE, NO OIL] This zesty version of my mom's cocktail sauce works well as a dip for appetizers like Tortilla "Fried" Mushrooms (page 68) or even crisp veggie sticks.

¼ cup catsup
1 tablespoon prepared horseradish
⅛ teaspoon freshly squeezed lemon
    juice (optional)

Place all of the ingredients in a small bowl. Stir to combine. Serve!

Aioli Dip with Baked Garlic

[MAKES 8 SERVINGS] [NUT FREE] The baked garlic adds jazzy-pizzazz to this vegan aioli. Eggless mayo makes this dip super creamy, but if you cannot find vegan mayo, you can use plain vegan yogurt or even whipped tofu instead. Adjust the seasoning accordingly.

---

7 cloves garlic, chopped
½ teaspoon extra-virgin olive oil
½ cup vegan mayonnaise
½ tablespoon freshly squeezed
    lemon juice
⅛ teaspoon sea salt

Preheat the oven to 350 degrees F. Put the chopped garlic and olive oil in a small ovenproof dish and stir to combine. Cover and bake for 20 to 25 minutes. Remove the garlic from the oven and allow it to cool for 20 minutes. Put the vegan mayonnaise, lemon juice, and salt in a small bowl. Add the garlic mixture and stir to combine. Serve as a dipping sauce.

Tortilla "Fried" Mushrooms

[MAKES 4 SERVINGS] [NUT FREE] Yum, yum, yum. One night I wanted to make an appetizer that I knew my husband would go crazy for and this is what I came up with. This delightful finger food mimics the fried mushrooms you might find on the menu at a fast-food chain, but these fabulous fungi are much lower in fat and super high on good flavor!

4 to 5 cups tortilla chips (spicy blue corn chips are nice)
⅛ teaspoon cayenne pepper
4 tablespoons vegan mayonnaise or plain vegan yogurt
16 ounces cremini or button mushrooms, cleaned and stemmed

Preheat the oven to 350 degrees F. Line a large, rimmed baking sheet with unbleached parchment paper. Put the tortilla chips and cayenne pepper in a blender and process into coarse crumbs. Put the tortilla crumbs in a medium bowl. Put the vegan mayonnaise or vegan yogurt in a small bowl.

Dip each mushroom into the vegan mayonnaise or vegan yogurt to liberally coat and then dip the mushroom in the tortilla mixture to coat with crumbs. Place each mushroom, round side up, on the prepared baking sheet. Continue in the same manner with all of the mushrooms.

Tent the mushrooms with foil and bake for 35 to 40 minutes. Remove the foil and bake for an additional 5 to 10 minutes until mushrooms are golden on top.

Jazzy Tip: Unbleached parchment paper is compostable and nontoxic, so it's a better choice than white parchment paper when creating your earth-friendly vegan creations.

Aioli Dip with Baked Garlic
(page 67)

Spicy Dip (page 67)

Tortilla "Fried" Mushrooms (opposite)

Party Potato Skins

[MAKES 3 TO 6 SERVINGS] [NUT FREE] My husband kept asking, "Why don't you make jazzy potato skins? Everyone will love them!" Let's face it, husbands aren't always right, but this time his suggestion was fabulous. These snazzy spuds make the perfect appetizer, light lunch, or jazzy snack.

3 very large russet potatoes, scrubbed, baked, and cooled (see note and see page 209)

1 teaspoon regular or smoked paprika

2 cups diced cremini mushroom caps

1 cup (about 1 medium) diced sweet red pepper

1 cup lightly packed, finely chopped baby spinach

⅓ cup minced onion

2 teaspoons all-purpose seasoning

1 teaspoon reduced-sodium tamari

1 teaspoon extra-virgin olive oil, plus more as needed

1 cup shredded vegan cheddar-style cheese (optional)

CHEF'S NOTE

The russet potatoes may be baked up to 24 to 36 hours in advance of preparing this recipe. After they have cooled, wrap them tightly in foil and store them in the refrigerator until use.

Preheat the oven to 375 degrees F. Line a large, rimmed baking sheet with unbleached parchment paper.

Slice each potato in half lengthwise. Carefully scoop out the pulp, using a teaspoon or grapefruit spoon, leaving about ¼ inch of the potato skin intact. (Reserve the pulp for another use.) Arrange the skins on the prepared baking sheet. Sprinkle the skins with ½ teaspoon paprika.

To make the filling, put the mushrooms, sweet pepper, spinach, onion, all-purpose seasoning, tamari, olive oil, and the remaining ½ teaspoon paprika in a medium bowl and stir until evenly coated. If the mixture seems dry, add a bit more olive oil.

Spoon one-sixth of the filling into each skin. Tent with foil and bake 35 to 40 minutes until the vegetables are soft. Remove the foil and bake 10 to 15 minutes. Add the vegan cheese (if using) and bake 10 minutes or until the vegan cheese is melted and the edges of the potatoes are crisp and golden. Put the potatoes on a large platter and cool for 5 to 10 minutes before serving.

To serve as an entrée, serve 2 to 3 skins per person. To serve as an appetizer course, serve 1 skin per person, cutting each skin into 3 to 4 slices right before serving.

Homemade Tortilla Chips

[MAKES 4 SERVINGS] [NUT FREE, NO OIL] You'll really impress with these quick-to-bake tortilla chips. They are so crispy and tasty that you will not miss the oil or the extra calories found in most store-bought varieties.

2 whole-grain tortillas (see notes)
½ teaspoon chili powder
¼ teaspoon sea salt, plus more as
  needed

CHEF'S NOTES

For a gluten-free option, use brown rice tortillas instead of whole-grain tortillas.

Flavored tortillas, like spinach or chipotle, work well in this recipe.

Preheat the oven to 400 degrees F. Line a large, rimmed baking sheet with unbleached parchment paper.

Cut tortillas into "chip"-size portions. Put the cut tortillas, chili powder, and salt in a large bowl. Toss to coat. Arrange the tortillas in a single layer on the prepared sheet. Bake 7 to 10 minutes or just until crisp and edges are slightly browned. Sprinkle with more salt, if desired.

Jazzy Tip: Whether you are packing a kid's lunch box or running your own daily errands, remember to bring a satisfying snack to help fulfill cravings when the munchies strike. Try creating a custom-made trail mix from your favorite organic nuts and seeds, dried fruits, and other preferred snack ingredients.

Beautiful Basil Lemonade

[MAKES 2 SERVINGS] [NUT FREE, NO OIL] Light, refreshing, and sweet, this summery treat will wow your taste buds with the unexpected flavor of fresh basil.

---

2 tablespoons freshly squeezed
    lemon juice
6 to 10 fresh basil leaves
1 tablespoon maple syrup, plus
    more as needed
16 ounces filtered or spring water
2 large sprigs fresh basil, for
    garnish (optional)

Put the lemon juice and basil leaves in a small bowl, and stir vigorously to combine, bruising basil leaves to release the flavor. Stir in maple syrup. Remove the basil leaves, and divide the lemon mixture into two tall, 16-ounce glasses.

Fill each glass with ice, then pour 8 ounces of water into each glass, stirring constantly. Stir well to combine. Garnish each glass with a sprig of basil leaves (if desired). Serve immediately.

Very-Berry Summer Tea

[MAKES 6 TO 8 SERVINGS] [NUT FREE, NO OIL] I make this tea all summer long and keep a large pitcher in the refrigerator. This icy delight is perfect for cooling off when summer thirst strikes. *So* refreshing! (Make sure to always make iced tea well ahead of time, so it can be served extra-cold for ideal taste.)

---

1 quart filtered or spring water
3 to 4 berry-flavored tea bags
2 tablespoons maple syrup, plus
    more as needed

Bring the water to a boil over high heat in a teakettle or large pot. Put the tea bags in the bottom of a teapot. Pour the boiling water over the bags, cover, and let steep for 15 to 25 minutes. Remove the tea bags. Add the maple syrup and stir to incorporate. Add more maple syrup, if desired, to taste. Let the tea cool completely. Transfer to a large pitcher. Refrigerate the tea for at least 4 hours. To serve, pour into tall glasses, add plenty of ice, and sip away!

Tofu Ranchero (page 81)

Chapter 5
Breakfast Favorites

How many times have you been asked:
What's for breakfast? Exchanging ordinary a.m.
fare for appealing new dishes can be challenging,
but in this chapter I'll share some of my favorite
recipes to wake up your good morning meal. From
my unique tofu-stuffed treat, Rocky Mountain
Toast (page 82), to a southwestern-inspired delight,
Tofu Ranchero (page 81), to a delectable breakfast
beverage, Raspberry-Tofu Smoothie (page 84), your
first meal of the day is going to rock! Add some
old-time family favorites, like granola and oatmeal,
cooked up jazzy style, and your breakfast recipe
lineup is complete. Top o' the morning to you!

"Making the simple complicated is commonplace; making the complicated simple, awesomely simple, that's creativity."

—Charles Mingus Jr.

Maple & Cherry Oatmeal

[MAKES 4 SERVINGS] [NUT FREE, NO OIL] I love oatmeal. I make it many ways, but this is one of my favorite versions of the well-loved breakfast classic.

OATMEAL
3¾ cups filtered or spring water
2 cups old-fashioned rolled oats
3 tablespoons dried cherries
⅛ teaspoon sea salt

TOPPINGS
1 tablespoon maple sugar, plus
    more as needed
Nondairy milk (optional)

Put all of the oatmeal ingredients in a medium sauce pan. Cover and bring to a simmer over medium-low heat. Simmer for 7 to 10 minutes. Uncover and sprinkle the maple sugar evenly over the top of the oatmeal. Cover, remove the pan from the heat, and let stand for 5 to 7 minutes before serving. Serve with nondairy milk (if using) and additional maple sugar on the side.

Coconut Oatmeal

[MAKES 2 SERVINGS] Here's a real jazzy twist on a breakfast staple.

1 cup rolled oats
1 cup nondairy milk, plus more as
    needed
1 cup filtered or spring water, plus
    more as needed
¼ cup dried cranberries
2 tablespoons unsweetened
    shredded dried coconut
¼ teaspoon ground cinnamon
Maple syrup (optional)

Put the oats, nondairy milk, water, cranberries, coconut, and cinnamon in a medium sauce pan. Cover and let the mixture soak at room temperature for 40 minutes. If the mixture absorbs most of the liquid, add 2 more tablespoons of water. Bring to a simmer over medium-low heat, cover and cook for about 7 minutes or until all of the liquid is absorbed. Remove from the heat and gently stir. Cover and let sit for 5 minutes before serving. Serve with more nondairy milk and maple syrup (if using).

Magnificent Maple Granola with Banana Whipped Topping

[MAKES 6 TO 8 SERVINGS] Nothin' like homemade granola. I love the scent and taste of freshly baked granola served with some nondairy milk on the side. To jazz it up a bit, top the granola with a dollop of Banana Whipped Topping (page 58). Mornings just got better!

2 cups rolled oats
¼ cup raw sunflower seeds
¼ cup raw pumpkin seeds
¼ cup raw unsweetened shredded dried coconut
¼ cup chopped walnuts
¼ cup raw or toasted wheat germ
1 teaspoon ground cinnamon
½ cup maple syrup
¾ cup raisins
Banana Whipped Topping (page 58) (optional)

Preheat the oven to 325 degrees F. Line a large, rimmed baking sheet with unbleached parchment paper.

Put the rolled oats, sunflower seeds, pumpkin seeds, coconut, walnuts, wheat germ, and cinnamon in a large bowl and stir to combine. Add the maple syrup and stir until evenly coated. Spread the mixture in an even layer on the lined baking sheet.

Bake for 17 to 20 minutes, stirring often. Add the raisins and bake 5 minutes more or until the oats are slightly golden. Transfer to a room temperature baking sheet and let cool for 30 minutes before serving. Serve with optional Banana Whipped Topping, if desired.

Chocolate Chip Granola

[MAKES 2 TO 3 SERVINGS] [NUT FREE] My husband just loves the pop of chocolate in this nut-free granola. If you prefer, you can use carob chips in place of the chocolate chips in this recipe. Great for an afternoon snack, too!

1 cup rolled oats
3 tablespoons maple syrup
½ teaspoon ground cinnamon
¼ teaspoon sea salt
½ cup raisins or dried cherries
⅓ cup vegan dark chocolate chips
   (preferably grain sweetened)

Preheat the oven to 350 degrees F. Line a large, rimmed baking sheet with unbleached parchment paper.

Put the rolled oats, maple syrup, cinnamon, and salt in a large bowl and stir until evenly coated. Spread the oats in an even layer on the lined baking sheet.

Bake for 20 minutes, stirring often. Add the raisins or cherries and chocolate chips and bake for 5 minutes or until the oats are golden and the chips start to melt. Transfer to a room temperature baking sheet or large bowl. Stir gently and allow to cool for at least 30 minutes before serving.

Tofu Ranchero

[MAKES 4 SERVINGS] [NUT FREE] Years ago my dad went out West to race his car in the Baja 500. While his race car actually never made it to the final race, Dad did emerge from the desert with one of my favorite breakfast recipes of all time. While plotting out his racecourse, he happened upon a remote restaurant that served an egg-based version of this recipe. My stepmom made the egg version for years, and now I am sharing my fabulous vegan re-do.

---

4 whole-grain tortillas
2 large or 3 medium tomatoes, roughly chopped
1 medium onion, sliced
1 teaspoon dried cilantro or 1 tablespoon chopped fresh cilantro
¼ teaspoon ground cumin
½ teaspoon extra-virgin olive oil (optional)
⅛ teaspoon cayenne pepper
⅛ teaspoon sea salt
1 yellow or orange sweet pepper, sliced
14 to 16 ounces firm or extra-firm regular tofu, drained
1 teaspoon turmeric
¼ teaspoon regular or reduced-sodium tamari

Preheat the oven to 375 degrees F. Wrap the tortillas in foil.

Put the tomatoes in a blender and process until the texture resembles a chunky sauce. Put the tomatoes, onion, cilantro, cumin, ¼ teaspoon of olive oil (if using), cayenne pepper, and salt in a large skillet. Bring to a simmer and cook for 7 minutes over medium-low heat. Add the sweet pepper, cover, and simmer for 5 to 7 minutes.

Put the tortillas in the oven and heat for 5 to 10 minutes or until they are warm.

Meanwhile, combine the tofu, turmeric, tamari, and the remaining ¼ teaspoon of olive oil (if using) in a medium bowl and mash with a potato masher or large fork until the tofu resembles the color and texture of cooked scrambled eggs. In a nonstick skillet, cook the tofu mixture for 5 to 7 minutes, or until heated through, stirring frequently.

Remove the tortillas from the oven. For each serving, place a tortilla on a large plate. Spoon one-quarter of the tofu mixture over the tortilla and then top with one-quarter of the tomato sauce. Serve immediately.

CHEF'S NOTE

For a gluten-free option, use gluten-free tortillas instead of whole-grain ones.

Rocky Mountain Toast

[MAKES 4 TO 6 SERVINGS] [NUT FREE] Just like moms used to make, sans the eggs. I say *moms* because it turns out that both my mother and my husband's mother made an egg-based version of this savory breakfast delicacy when we were young. If you try it once, you'll be hooked!

4 to 6 slices whole-grain bread (see note)
1 tablespoon vegan margarine
14 to 16 ounces firm or extra-firm regular tofu, drained
½ cup shredded vegan cheese
½ teaspoon turmeric
¼ teaspoon tamari
⅛ teaspoon sea salt
⅛ teaspoon freshly ground pepper (optional)

— CHEF'S NOTE —

For a gluten-free option, use a gluten-free bread in this recipe.

Put a bread slice on a cutting board. Cut a hole in the center of the bread, about 3 inches in diameter, using a bread knife or cookie cutter. Repeat with all of the bread slices. (Reserve the bread "middles" to make bread crumbs for another meal.) Spread a bit of vegan margarine on each side of the bread. Set 2 to 3 bread slices in a large, nonstick skillet. Turn the heat to medium-low and let the slices begin to brown on one side.

Meanwhile, put the tofu in a medium bowl and mash with a potato masher or large fork until crumbly. Add the vegan cheese, turmeric, tamari, salt, and pepper (if using). Mash until the tofu resembles the color and texture of cooked scrambled eggs.

Scoop up one-quarter of the tofu mixture and place it in the center of each bread slice in the skillet. Pat down firmly with a flat spatula until the filling becomes compact. Cook for 2 to 3 minutes and then flip. Cover and cook on the other side for 5 to 7 minutes, or until the bread is golden and crispy and the tofu mixture is warmed through. Keep warm in a 300 degrees F oven. Repeat with the other bread slices. Serve immediately with fresh fruit on the side.

Raspberry-Tofu Smoothie

[MAKES 1 SERVING] [NUT FREE, NO OIL] This smoothie is appetizing, thick, rich, and creamy. If you add less nondairy milk, and a bit more maple syrup, it makes a refreshing vegan frozen dessert—my favorite!

¾ cup frozen raspberries (see note and Jazzy Tips below)
½ cup (about 4 ounces) soft silken tofu
1½ tablespoons maple syrup
⅓ cup nondairy milk, plus more as needed

Put all of the ingredients in a blender and process until very smooth, adding more nondairy milk as needed to achieve the desired consistency. Serve immediately.

—— CHEF'S NOTE ——

Frozen blueberries or strawberries may be substituted for the raspberries, if desired.

Jazzy Tips:

Freezing Berries: It's easy to freeze fresh berries. Wash them well, and dry on clean kitchen towels. Then put them in a resealable freezer bag. Seal bag well and freeze for at least 12 hours before using.

Freezing Bananas: To freeze bananas, peel, then break each one into 3 or 4 pieces and put them in a resealable freezer bag. Seal and freeze for at least 12 hours before using.

Blueberry Green Smoothie

[MAKES 2 SERVINGS] [NUT FREE, NO OIL] Smoothies make a fabulous breakfast refresher or afternoon snack. This one makes great use of blueberries when they are in season, but the frozen variety works perfectly, too!

2 frozen bananas (see Jazzy Tips, page 84)

1½ cups frozen blueberries (see Jazzy Tips, page 84)

½ cup lightly packed baby spinach

2 tablespoons maple syrup, plus more as needed

1 cup filtered or spring water, plus more as needed

Put all of the ingredients in a blender. Process until smooth and creamy, adding more water as needed to achieve the desired consistency. Add more maple syrup if a sweeter flavor is desired. Serve immediately.

Banana-Raspberry Breakfast Smoothie

[MAKES 2 SERVINGS] [NUT FREE, NO OIL] This is one of my favorite smoothie combos.

2 fresh or frozen bananas (see Jazzy Tips, page 84)

1½ cups frozen raspberries (see Jazzy Tips, page 84)

2 pitted Medjool dates

1 cup filtered or spring water, plus more as needed

1 tablespoon maple syrup

Put all of the ingredients in a blender. Process until smooth, adding more water as needed to achieve the desired consistency. Serve immediately.

Pineapple-Banana-Strawberry Smoothie

[MAKES 2 TO 3 SERVINGS] [NUT FREE, NO OIL] Sweet pineapple and plump strawberries combine to make a delectable smoothie combination. If you prefer agave syrup, you can use it instead of the maple syrup in this recipe.

2 very large frozen bananas (see Jazzy Tips, page 84)

2 cups chilled nondairy milk, plus more as needed (vanilla variety is preferable)

1½ cups cubed pineapple, chilled

1 cup frozen strawberries (see Jazzy Tips, page 84)

1 tablespoon maple syrup (optional), plus more as needed

Put all of the ingredients in a blender and process until smooth and creamy. Taste and add more nondairy milk or maple syrup, if desired. Pour the mixture into pretty glasses. Serve immediately.

CHEF'S NOTE

For an extra pop of nutrition, add a handful of baby spinach before blending—it's a great way to get kids to eat their greens!

Cranberry-Pecan Quick Biscuits (page 101)

Chapter 6

Marvelous Muffins

Muffins are marvelous and that is why I have devoted an entire chapter to these timeless baked treats! Muffins may be savory or they may be sweet. Muffins may be giant or mini-size. Muffins may be served for breakfast, lunch, dinner, or an in-between snack. Muffins travel well and are ideal for packing in a lunchbox or a picnic lunch, or as an on-the-go quick bite. No wonder I love muffins so much!

"Jazz is about
being in the moment."
——Herbie Hancock

Coconut Chocolate Chip Muffins

[MAKES 6 MUFFINS] The chocolate and coconut both help to bind these muffins, so no egg is needed. With minimal ingredients required, these tasty treats whip up fast and are ideal for an afternoon snack or quick dessert.

1½ cups whole-wheat pastry flour
½ cup raw unsweetened shredded dried coconut
1 teaspoon baking soda
1 teaspoon baking powder
¼ teaspoon sea salt
½ cup firmly packed brown sugar
1 cup, plus 2 tablespoons nondairy milk
2 teaspoons freshly squeezed lemon juice
½ cup vegan dark chocolate chips

Preheat the oven to 375 degrees F. Line a six-cup standard muffin tin with paper liners. Put the flour, coconut, baking soda, baking powder, and salt in a large bowl and stir with a dry whisk to combine. Add the brown sugar and stir with the whisk to combine. Stir in the nondairy milk and the lemon juice. Stir in the chocolate chips.

Mound the mixture into the prepared muffin cups. Put the muffin tin on a rimmed baking sheet and bake for 30 to 40 minutes, or until golden and a toothpick inserted in the middle of a muffin comes out clean. Put the muffin tin on a wire rack and loosen the sides of the muffins with a knife. Let cool for about 15 minutes. Carefully remove the muffins from the muffin tin, and let cool for 30 minutes. Serve warm or at room temperature. The muffins will keep for up to 2 days stored tightly covered in the refrigerator.

Jazzy Tip: Instead of using processed white sugar (which is sometimes whitened by being filtered through animal bone char) or honey (yes, it is an animal product, made by bees), try using organic maple syrup or maple sugar when baking. These savvy sweeteners produce a delicate but satisfying sweet taste to your sugary baked treats.

Apple Muffins with Pumpkin Seeds

[MAKES 6 MUFFINS] Sweet, moist, and packed with the slightly tart taste of apples, these muffins make a wonderful breakfast treat, lunch companion, or afternoon snack. Freshly puréed apples stand in for all of the oil and some of the sugar, making these baked gems low in fat but high in flavor.

2 cups whole-wheat flour
1 teaspoon baking powder
1 teaspoon baking soda
1 teaspoon ground cinnamon
⅛ teaspoon sea salt
1 cup raisins
½ cup raw pumpkin seeds
1½ cups fresh apple purée (see note)
1 tablespoon freshly squeezed
    lemon juice
1 teaspoon lemon zest
⅓ cup maple syrup
½ cup nondairy milk, plus more as
    needed

—— CHEF'S NOTE ——

To make apple purée, peel and core three very large or four medium apples. Rough chop the apples. Put the apples in a blender and process until the consistency of smooth applesauce is achieved. Be careful not to liquefy!

Preheat the oven to 375 degrees F. Oil a six-cup standard muffin tin. Put the flour, baking powder, baking soda, cinnamon, and salt in a large bowl and stir with a dry whisk to combine. Add the raisins and pumpkin seeds and stir to coat. Stir in the apple purée.

Stir in the lemon juice, lemon zest, maple syrup, and nondairy milk, and mix just until incorporated. The batter will be quite thick, but if it seems overly dry, stir in a bit more nondairy milk, 1 tablespoon at a time, until the mixture is moist. Don't overmix or the muffins will be tough.

Mound the mixture into the prepared muffin cups. Put the muffin tin on a baking sheet and bake for 35 to 40 minutes, or until golden and a toothpick inserted in the center of a muffin comes out clean. Put the muffin tin on a wire rack and loosen the sides of each muffin with a knife. Let cool for about 15 minutes. Carefully remove the muffins. Serve warm or at room temperature.

Strawberry Surprise Apple Muffins

[MAKES 6 GIANT MUFFINS] [NUT FREE, NO OIL] These tasty treats make the perfect lunchbox companion or snazzy after-school snack. The strawberry filling offers a surprise pop of flavor and fun. The apple purée takes the place of both the oil *and* the egg! This mouthwatering muffin is also low in fat and lower in sugar than most commercial varieties.

---

2 cups whole-wheat flour
1 teaspoon baking powder
1 teaspoon baking soda
1 teaspoon ground cinnamon
⅛ teaspoon sea salt
1 cup raisins
1½ cups fresh apple purée (see note, page 93)
1 tablespoon freshly squeezed lemon juice
⅓ cup maple syrup
½ cup vanilla-flavored nondairy milk, plus more as needed
1 teaspoon vanilla extract
6 heaping teaspoons whole-fruit strawberry preserves, excess liquid drained off

Preheat the oven to 375 degrees F. Line a six-cup standard muffin tin with paper liners. Put the flour, baking powder, baking soda, cinnamon, and salt in a large bowl and stir with a dry whisk to combine. Add the raisins and stir to coat. Stir in the apple purée. Stir in the lemon juice, maple syrup, nondairy milk, and vanilla extract, and mix just until incorporated. The batter will be quite thick, but if it seems overly dry, stir in more nondairy milk, 1 tablespoon at a time. Don't overmix.

Mound half of the mixture into the prepared muffin cups. Spoon 1 heaping teaspoon of the preserves into the center of each muffin. Top each muffin with the remaining batter, evenly distributing it among the six muffin cups.

Put the muffin tin on a rimmed baking sheet and bake for 35 to 40 minutes, or until golden and a toothpick inserted in the side of a muffin comes out clean. Put the muffin tin on a wire rack and loosen the sides of each muffin with a knife. Let cool for about 15 minutes. Carefully remove the muffins.

Zucchini-Raspberry Muffins

[MAKES 6 MUFFINS] [NUT FREE, NO OIL] Zucchini, zucchini, zucchini. Do you ever wonder what to do with all of that lovely zucchini that you may find at your local farmers' market at summer's end? Here is a way to transform this shiny-skinned squash into a sweet treat that your whole family will savor.

2 cups fresh or frozen raspberries
1½ cups nondairy milk, plus more
    as needed
2 cups whole-wheat flour
2 teaspoons baking powder
1 teaspoon baking soda
1 teaspoon ground cinnamon
¼ teaspoon sea salt
⅓ cup brown sugar
⅓ cup toasted wheat germ
1 cup raisins
1 cup shredded raw zucchini, drained
    (see note, page 100)

Preheat the oven to 375 degrees F. Line a six-cup standard muffin tin with paper liners. Put the raspberries and nondairy milk in a blender and process until smooth.

Put the flour, baking powder, baking soda, cinnamon, and salt in a large bowl and stir with a dry whisk to combine. Add the brown sugar and wheat germ, and stir to combine. Add the raisins and stir to coat. Stir in the shredded raw zucchini. Stir in the blended raspberry mixture and mix just until incorporated. The batter will be quite thick, but if it seems overly dry, stir in a bit more nondairy milk, 1 tablespoon at a time, until the mixture is moist. Don't overmix or the muffins will be tough.

Mound the mixture into the prepared muffin cups. Put the muffin tin on a rimmed baking sheet and bake for 35 to 40 minutes, or until golden and a toothpick inserted in the center of a muffin comes out clean. Put the muffin tin on a wire rack and loosen the sides of each muffin with a knife. Let cool for about 15 minutes. Carefully remove the muffins. Serve warm or at room temperature.

Cornbread and Sweet Pepper Mini-Muffins

[MAKES 12 MINI-MUFFINS] [NUT FREE] Here is a muffin recipe that will certainly impress. Savory and slightly sweet, these mini jewels pair well with a first-course salad or soup, but they work great as breakfast muffins, too. The peppers add a welcome pop of color and taste, while the cornmeal adds a hearty texture.

½ cup plus 3 tablespoons fine-ground cornmeal, plus more as needed (see note)
½ cup whole-wheat flour
½ teaspoon baking powder
¼ teaspoon sea salt
½ cup diced sweet red pepper
1 cup sliced banana
⅓ cup nondairy milk
¼ teaspoon chili powder
¼ cup maple syrup

CHEF'S NOTE

Make sure to use fine-ground cornmeal, not coarse-ground cornmeal, or your muffins will be inedible!

Preheat the oven to 400 degrees F. Oil a twelve-cup mini-muffin tin. Put the cornmeal, flour, baking powder, and salt in a large bowl and stir with a dry whisk to combine. Add the red pepper and stir gently to coat.

Put the banana, nondairy milk, and chili powder in a blender. Process until the mixture is smooth. Pour the banana mixture into the flour mixture and stir just until incorporated. Add the maple syrup and stir briefly to incorporate. The batter should be quite thick. If the mixture seems too runny, gently stir in more cornmeal, 1 heaping teaspoon at a time, to achieve a thick batter that holds soft peaks when stirred.

Divide the mixture among the prepared muffin cups. Bake for 20 to 25 minutes, or until golden and a toothpick inserted in the center of a muffin comes out clean. Put the muffin tin on a wire rack and loosen the sides of each muffin with a knife. Cool for about 10 minutes. Carefully remove the muffins. Serve warm or at room temperature.

Cinnamon-Maple Mini-Muffins

[MAKES 12 MINI-MUFFINS] [NUT FREE] The quintessential quick bread, these cinnamon beauties pair well at any meal and at snack time, too! A bonus: they are so easy to prepare!

1 cup whole-wheat flour
1 teaspoon baking powder
½ teaspoon ground cinnamon
⅛ teaspoon sea salt
½ cup raisins
⅓ cup plus 1 teaspoon nondairy milk
⅓ cup maple syrup
1 tablespoon extra-virgin olive oil

Preheat the oven to 375 degrees F. Oil a twelve-cup mini-muffin tin. Put the flour, baking powder, cinnamon, and salt in a large bowl and stir with a dry whisk to combine. Stir in the raisins. Stir in the nondairy milk, maple syrup, and olive oil, and mix just until incorporated. The batter will be quite thick. Don't overmix or the muffins will be tough.

Divide the mixture among the prepared muffin cups. Bake for 25 to 35 minutes, or until golden and a toothpick inserted in the center of a muffin comes out clean. Put the muffin tin on a wire rack. Let cool for about 15 minutes. Carefully remove the muffins. Serve warm or at room temperature.

Blueberry-Zucchini Mini-Muffins

[MAKES 12 MINI-MUFFINS] [NUT FREE, NO OIL] The blueberry preserves add a neat surprise in the middle of these delicious baked delights. Pack them in a lunch box or picnic basket for a welcome addition to any traveling meal, or serve them warm, right out of the oven, for a special breakfast treat.

1 cup whole-wheat flour
1 teaspoon baking powder
1 teaspoon baking soda
¼ teaspoon sea salt
⅓ cup brown sugar
1 teaspoon freshly squeezed
    lemon juice
½ cup nondairy milk, plus more
    as needed
¾ cup grated zucchini, drained
    (see note)
⅓ cup raisins
12 teaspoons whole-fruit blueberry
    preserves, excess liquid drained off

CHEF'S NOTE

You can press out excess liquid from the shredded zucchini by putting it in a fine mesh colander and placing it over a medium bowl. Let the zucchini drain for 5 to 10 minutes, and then gently press the excess liquid out into the bowl using a soft spatula.

Preheat the oven to 375 degrees F. Line a twelve-cup mini-muffin tin with paper liners.

Put the flour, baking powder, baking soda, and salt in a large bowl and stir with a dry whisk to combine. Add the brown sugar and stir with the whisk to combine. Stir in the lemon juice and nondairy milk, and mix just until incorporated. Stir in the zucchini and raisins. The batter will be quite thick, but if it seems overly dry, stir in a bit more nondairy milk, 1 tablespoon at a time. Don't overmix or the muffins will be tough.

Mound half of the batter into the prepared mini-muffin cups. Spoon 1 teaspoon of the preserves into the center of each muffin. Top each muffin cup with the remaining half of the batter, evenly distributing it among the twelve muffin cups.

Put the muffin tin on a baking sheet and bake for 20 to 30 minutes, or until golden and a toothpick inserted in the middle of a muffin comes out clean. Put the muffin tin on a wire rack. Let cool for about 15 minutes. Carefully remove the muffins. Serve warm or at room temperature.

Cranberry-Pecan Quick Biscuits

[MAKES 12 MINI-BISCUITS] I love cranberries. I love pecans. Mix 'em together with a few other ingredients and you have a crunchy, tart, and sweet treat to serve as a breakfast side, satisfying snack, or excellent complement to a soup or salad.

1 cup plus 2 tablespoons whole-wheat flour
1 teaspoon baking powder
½ teaspoon baking soda
1 teaspoon ground cinnamon
⅔ cup dried cranberries
½ cup plus 2 tablespoons chopped pecans
⅓ cup vanilla-flavored nondairy milk
⅓ cup maple syrup

Preheat the oven to 400 degrees F. Oil a twelve-cup mini-muffin tin.

Put the flour, baking powder, baking soda, and cinnamon in a large bowl and stir with a dry whisk to combine. Stir in the cranberries and pecans. Stir in the nondairy milk and maple syrup. Mix just until incorporated. The batter will be quite thick. Don't overmix or the biscuits will be tough.

Divide the mixture among the prepared muffin cups. Bake for 20 to 25 minutes, or until golden and a toothpick inserted in the center of a biscuit comes out clean. Put the muffin tin on a wire rack and loosen the sides of each biscuit with a knife. Cool for about 5 minutes. Carefully remove the biscuits. Cool 10 minutes more. Serve warm or at room temperature.

Creamy Cauliflower Bisque (page 111)

Chapter 7

Soups, Bisques, and Stews

I think soup is the perfect food. Soups can be served as impressive starters, as light entrées, or as a hearty main course. Delicate first-course bisques can whet appetites while enhancing an elegant dinner menu. A thick and robust stew is an appealing one-pot meal to serve for big appetites when time is at a premium. No matter how you say it, a great soup is truly the cornerstone of a complete and satisfying meal!

"Next to jazz music, there is nothing that lifts the spirit and strengthens the soul more than a good bowl of chili."

—Harry James

Four-Ingredient Leek Soup

[MAKES 4 SERVINGS] [NUT FREE] Delicate and light, this quick-to-make soup packs a punch of flavor and tantalizing texture. It makes perfect first-course fare for an elegant soirée or it may be served as a light luncheon entrée with a nice salad on the side.

1 large bunch leeks (include light green parts), cleaned well and thinly sliced
2 teaspoons extra-virgin olive oil
4 cups vegetable broth
½ teaspoon all-purpose seasoning

Put the leeks, olive oil, and 2 tablespoons of the vegetable broth in a skillet. Cook over medium-low heat for about 5 minutes until the leeks are soft. Add more broth, 1 tablespoon at a time, if leeks become dry. Add the remaining broth and seasoning. Bring to a boil over medium heat. Decrease the heat to medium-low and cook for 10 minutes. Serve immediately.

Jazzy Tip: Leeks must be cleaned thoroughly to remove the fine sand and dirt often embedded between the layers. When you are using sliced leeks in a recipe, here's a quick and easy way to do the job: Slice the leeks. Put them in a large bowl filled with cold water and swish briefly with your hands to loosen any debris. Transfer them to a colander and rinse under cold water so the debris rinses away. Put the leeks in a clean bowl of cold water and swish to remove any remaining sand or dirt. Transfer them back to the colander, rinse under cold water, and drain well.

Creamy Broccoli Soup

[MAKES 3 TO 4 SERVINGS] [NUT FREE, NO OIL] This delicate, tummy-warming soup makes a lovely light lunch or an ideal starter course for a formal soirée.

---

6 cups broccoli florets
1 clove garlic, chopped
2 cups cold nondairy milk, plus
    more as needed
1 teaspoon regular or reduced-
    sodium tamari (to taste)
1 teaspoon all-purpose seasoning
¼ teaspoon sea salt
Pinch of cayenne pepper
Freshly ground pepper, to taste

Fit a steamer basket into a medium sauce pan with a tight-fitting lid. Add 2 inches of cold water, then add the broccoli. Cover and bring to a boil. Steam the broccoli until crisp-tender, about 7 minutes.

Put the steamed broccoli, garlic, nondairy milk, tamari, all-purpose seasoning, salt, and cayenne pepper in a blender and process on low until smooth, making sure to leave air space at top of blender to allow steam to escape. If the soup is too thick, add more nondairy milk, 2 tablespoons at a time, to achieve the desired consistency, pulsing or blending briefly after each addition.

Put the soup in a medium soup pot and cook over medium-low heat, until heated through, stirring often. Season with pepper. If soup is too thick, add more nondairy milk.

Serve immediately in deep soup bowls with whole-grain crackers or crusty bread on the side.

Chilled Avocado Soup

[MAKES 4 TO 6 SERVINGS] [NUT FREE] The creamy texture of the avocados in this chilled summer soup is enhanced by soft tofu, which stands in for the heavy cream so often called for in cold soups. It is a refreshing starter or entrée when the temperature is on the rise!

2 small avocados

12 ounces soft regular or silken tofu, drained and cubed

¼ sweet onion, chopped

2 tablespoons freshly squeezed lemon juice

1 small clove garlic, chopped

1 heaping teaspoon maple sugar

½ teaspoon chopped fresh cilantro

¼ teaspoon sea salt, plus more as needed

⅛ teaspoon cayenne pepper

2 tablespoons filtered or spring water, plus more as needed

Freshly ground pepper, to taste

Cilantro sprigs or chopped fresh flat-leaf parsley, for garnish

Peel, pit, and chop the avocados (see note). Put the chopped avocados, tofu, onion, lemon juice, garlic, maple sugar, cilantro, salt, cayenne pepper, and 2 tablespoons water in a blender and process until creamy. If the soup is too thick, add more water, 2 tablespoons at a time, up to ½ cup, to achieve the desired consistency. Transfer to a bowl. Season with additional salt and pepper if desired. Cover and refrigerate for 4 to 6 hours.

About 30 minutes before serving, chill four small soup bowls or six demitasse cups. To serve, ladle the soup into the chilled bowls. Garnish each serving with cilantro or parsley. Serve immediately.

CHEF'S NOTE

To prepare an avocado, use a sharp knife to cut the avocado in half lengthwise, gently inserting the knife and working your way around the pit. Using your hands, twist to separate the two halves, which will leave the pit intact. Use a spoon to gently remove the pit, then scoop the flesh from each half of the avocado. Since avocados brown quickly when exposed to air, prepare them immediately before serving.

Butternut Squash and White Bean Soup

[MAKES 10 TO 12 SERVINGS] [NUT FREE, NO OIL] Butternut squash truly adds a buttery taste to this delicious soup. Hearty and filling, this savory entrée will please even the most discerning palates.

8 cups low-fat vegetable broth

5 to 6 white potatoes, peeled and cubed

1 small butternut squash, peeled, seeded, and cubed

6 carrots, peeled and sliced

4 stalks celery with tops, sliced

1 teaspoon regular or reduced-sodium tamari

1 teaspoon all-purpose seasoning

¼ teaspoon garlic powder

1 heaping teaspoon brown sugar (optional)

2 to 3 cups filtered or spring water, plus more as needed

Several grinds of freshly ground pepper (optional)

1 can (15 ounces) white beans, drained and rinsed

Put all of the ingredients except for the white beans in a large soup pot. Add more water as needed to cover the vegetables by ¼ inch. Cover and cook over medium-low heat for 50 minutes to 1 hour. Add the white beans, and cook 15 minutes more. Spoon into soup bowls and serve piping hot.

Creamy Cauliflower Bisque

[MAKES 4 SERVINGS] [NUT FREE, NO OIL] Creamy is the operative word for this opulent offering. Steamed cauliflower harmonized with nondairy milk and other savory seasonings makes for a bisque that will prompt your diners to query, "Is there any dairy in this soup?"

---

1 medium head cauliflower, cut into florets
1 cup vegetable broth, plus more as needed
¼ cup plus 2 tablespoons unsweetened nondairy milk, plus more as needed
½ teaspoon ground cumin
¼ teaspoon sea salt
⅛ teaspoon freshly ground pepper (optional)

Fit a steamer basket into a medium sauce pan with a tight-fitting lid. Add 2 inches of cold water, then add the cauliflower. Cover and bring to a boil. Steam the cauliflower florets for about 20 minutes until tender.

Put the cauliflower, vegetable broth, nondairy milk, cumin, salt, and pepper (if using) in a blender and process until smooth. Add more broth or nondairy milk, ¼ cup at a time, to achieve the desired consistency.

Pour into a medium sauce pan, cover and cook over medium heat for about 10 minutes, stirring often, until heated through. Serve piping hot.

CHEF'S NOTE

After the soup is blended it may be cooled thoroughly, packed in a tightly sealed container, and stored in the refrigerator for up to 24 hours. To serve, pour into a medium sauce pan, cover, and simmer over medium-low heat for about 20 minutes, stirring often, until heated through.

Best Butternut Bisque

[MAKES 6 TO 8 SERVINGS] [NUT FREE, NO OIL] Thick and creamy in texture, this bisque is a true showstopper, perfect for any cold-weather meal. Whether presented as an elegant first course, hearty luncheon entrée, or main dish supper soup, the butternut squash assures a velvety consistency and buttery taste.

6 cups cubed butternut squash (1-inch cubes)

4 cups cauliflower florets

½ cup chopped onion (about 1 small onion)

1 teaspoon Italian or all-purpose seasoning

2 apples, peeled and chopped

1 teaspoon ground cinnamon

¼ teaspoon ground ginger

¼ teaspoon sea salt

2½ cups vegetable broth, plus more as needed

2 tablespoons maple syrup

CHEF'S NOTE

To reheat the soup, pour it into a pot. If soup seems too thick add more vegetable broth, to taste. Cook for about 15 minutes over medium-low heat, stirring often, until heated through.

Fit a steamer basket into a large pot with a tight-fitting lid. Add 2 inches of cold water, then add the squash. Cover, bring to a boil, and steam for 7 minutes. Add the cauliflower and onion. Sprinkle with the Italian or all-purpose seasoning and steam for 20 minutes or until the squash and cauliflower are both very soft.

Put the squash mixture in a large bowl. Let cool for 15 minutes. Add the apples, cinnamon, ginger, and salt and stir to coat. Put half of the mixture in a blender. Add 1¼ cups vegetable broth and 1 tablespoon maple syrup and process until smooth. Pour into a soup pot. Put the second half of the squash mixture in the blender. Add the remaining 1¼ cups vegetable broth and 1 tablespoon maple syrup, and process until smooth. Add to the soup pot, and then stir the two batches together. If the soup seems too thick, add more vegetable broth to taste. Put the pot over medium-low heat, cover, and simmer, stirring often, until heated through, about 10 minutes. To serve, ladle the soup into bowls.

This soup may be made up to 24 hours ahead of time. If making in advance, let the soup cool after blending, then pour the cooled soup into an airtight container and refrigerate (see note).

Rockin' Moroccan Stew

[MAKES 6 TO 8 SERVINGS] [NUT FREE, NO OIL] This stew really rocks. A hearty one-pot meal that bakes in the oven, it is easy to prepare, making it ideal to serve for a weeknight supper. However, its robust flavors and beautiful colors also make it fancy enough for a casual dinner party, served with brown rice or quinoa, crusty fresh bread, and a crisp green salad on the side.

1 large red onion, chopped
4 large carrots, peeled and cut in 1-inch slices
4 small (or 3 large) russet potatoes, peeled and cut in 1-inch cubes
1 small cauliflower, cut in florets
1 medium eggplant, peeled and cut in 1-inch cubes
1 can (15 ounces) chickpeas (garbanzo beans), drained and rinsed
1 can (28 ounces) crushed tomatoes
1 teaspoon ground cumin
1 teaspoon ground cinnamon
½ teaspoon cayenne pepper (or less to taste)
¼ teaspoon sea salt
2½ cups vegetable broth, plus more as needed

Preheat the oven to 375 degrees F. Put the onion, carrots, potatoes, cauliflower, eggplant, chickpeas, tomatoes, cumin, cinnamon, cayenne pepper, and salt in a large mixing bowl. Toss to combine.

Put the vegetable mixture in a 5- to 6-quart casserole dish or Dutch oven. Pour the vegetable broth over the top. Cover and bake for 1 hour 10 minutes to 1 hour 20 minutes or until the vegetables are soft. As the stew cooks, check it every half hour. If the stew becomes dry, add ¼ cup more vegetable broth as needed.

Remove the stew from the oven and let cool for 10 minutes. To serve, spoon the stew into deep soup bowls. Serve hot.

Caesar Salad, Jazzy-Style (page 120)

Mushroom-Nut Burgers (page 185)

Banana Milk-less Shake (page 255)

Chapter 8

Standout Salads

Eat your daily greens.
Hmm . . . sometimes easier said than
done, right? I am always on the lookout
to create fresh and delicious ways to wake
up my daily dose of leafy greens. I love to
add fancy fixings like lots of fresh veggies,
dried fruits, beans, grains, seeds, nuts, and
various plant-based proteins for a little
extra zest and zing! Top it off with a tasty,
tangy salad dressing and you have a
meal in a bowl. Yum.

"So, if I'm cooking,
I'll be steaming vegetables,
making some nice salad,
that kind of stuff."
—Sir Paul McCartney

Fancy Peeled Salad

[MAKES 6 SERVINGS] When a fancy dish is on the agenda, this combination of pretty peeled carrots and zucchini makes the perfect option. Kalamata olives provide a unique flavor, while artichoke hearts add substance to this show-stopping salad.

6 cups romaine lettuce, torn into bite-size pieces
1 avocado, peeled and sliced
1 small zucchini (unpeeled), washed and thinly sliced using a carrot peeler
2 carrots, scrubbed and thinly sliced using a carrot peeler
8 ounces marinated artichoke hearts, drained

12 to 14 pitted green or kalamata olives
½ cup minced sweet or red onion (about 1 small onion)
2 tablespoons Very Balsamic Salad Dressing (page 54), plus more as needed
3 tablespoons of Pumpkin Seed Parmesan (page 57) (optional)

Put the romaine, avocado, zucchini, carrots, artichoke hearts, olives, and onion in a large bowl. Pour the desired amount of dressing over top. Gently toss the salad. Sprinkle the top with Pumpkin Seed Parmesan (if using). Serve.

Jazzy Tip: Most of us want to get at least one big salad into our daily menu plan. But if you are anything like me, making the salad can be too time-consuming to do at the last minute. I like to wash salad greens ahead of time, so that they're ready to use when I need them. After the greens are washed and spun dry, place them in a large bowl with a paper towel on top. Cover and refrigerate. Your greens will be super crisp and ready to toss into your salad at suppertime.

Caesar Salad, Jazzy-Style

[MAKES 4 TO 6 SERVINGS] This vegan version of a traditional favorite adds a classic flair to any meal. Freshly prepared croutons add a real punch and tofu imparts a creamy consistency to the delightfully authentic-tasting dressing.

12 cups lightly packed romaine lettuce, washed, dried, and cut into bite-size pieces

CROUTONS
5 to 6 slices very fresh whole-grain bread
1 teaspoon garlic powder
1 tablespoon Italian seasoning

Caesar Salad Dressing (page 52)
1 tablespoon Cashew Parmesan (page 57), plus more for serving (optional)

CHEF'S NOTE

[NO OIL] For a completely oil-free recipe, omit the Cashew Parmesan.

Cover and refrigerate the prepared lettuce to allow it to crisp up.

Preheat the oven to 400 degrees F. Line a large, rimmed baking sheet with unbleached parchment paper. Cut each slice of bread into nine equally sized pieces. Put the bread cubes and garlic powder into a medium bowl, and stir gently to evenly coat the bread cubes. Add the Italian seasoning, and stir to evenly coat. Spread the seasoned bread cubes in an even layer on the prepared baking sheet.

Bake for 12 to 15 minutes, turning once, until the bread cubes are golden and crisp. Put the baking sheet on a wire rack. Let the croutons cool for 5 to 10 minutes.

Place the dressing in a large bowl. Add lettuce and croutons. Toss well to thoroughly coat the lettuce and croutons with the dressing. Sprinkle with Cashew Parmesan (if using). Serve immediately with more optional Cashew Parmesan on the side.

Quick Tomato Salad

Quick Tomato Salad

[MAKES 2 TO 3 SERVINGS] [NUT FREE, NO OIL] This is one of my summer staples, perfect to serve when tomatoes are at the height of their season and readily available at my local farmers' market. You'll be surprised at its full-bodied flavor even though it's only using a few very simple and basic ingredients.

---

1 pint grape or cherry tomatoes, halved
2 to 3 small cloves garlic, minced
⅛ teaspoon sea salt
Several grinds of freshly ground pepper

Put the tomatoes in a medium bowl. With clean hands or the back of a rubber spatula, lightly squeeze the tomatoes to release their juices. Stir in the garlic, sea salt, and fresh pepper. Let sit at room temperature for 5 to 20 minutes and serve.

Quick Baby Spinach Salad

[MAKES 2 TO 3 SERVINGS] [NUT FREE, NO OIL] The title says it all. A spinach salad that is quick and easy and packed with great taste.

---

3 cups lightly packed baby spinach
2 teaspoons balsamic vinegar
1 teaspoon maple syrup
Sea salt or Himalayan pink salt, to taste
Freshly ground pepper, to taste

Put the spinach in a medium bowl. To make the dressing, put the vinegar and maple syrup in a small bowl and briskly whisk until smooth. Pour the dressing over the spinach and toss gently to coat the leaves. Top with salt and pepper as desired.

Spinach and Apple Salad with Maple-Mustard Dressing

[MAKES 4 SERVINGS] Apples add a tart and sweet taste to the delicate baby spinach in this appetizing salad. Raisins and pumpkin seeds provide texture and flavor, while the dressing adds real zing!

Maple-Mustard Dressing (page 51)

SALAD
8 cups lightly packed baby spinach
1 large apple, peeled and thinly sliced
3 tablespoons raisins
2 tablespoons pumpkin seeds
Sea salt, to taste (optional)
Freshly ground pepper, to taste (optional)

Put the spinach, apple slices, raisins, and pumpkin seeds in a large bowl. Pour 4 tablespoons of the dressing over the spinach and toss gently to coat the leaves. Taste and add more dressing, salt, and pepper, if desired.

CHEF'S NOTE

When you make the dressing recipe, it may make more than you'll use for this salad, but it's a great basic dressing to have on hand. Stored in an airtight container in the refrigerator, leftover dressing will keep for about 3 days. Just whisk it briskly before using.

Festive Kale Salad

[MAKES 2 TO 4 SERVINGS] This slightly sweet and crunchy combination makes a satisfying luncheon salad or festive first course for a holiday meal. The lemon tenderizes the kale, transforming it into a delightful alternative to your everyday green salad. Pair this appealing dish with crusty bread to enhance the delicate flavors.

DRESSING
3 tablespoons freshly squeezed
    lemon juice
3 tablespoons maple syrup

SALAD
6 to 8 cups very thinly sliced, lightly
    packed curly kale, washed and
    dried
½ cup dried cranberries or dried
    cherries
⅓ cup chopped walnuts
Sea salt, to taste (optional)
Freshly ground pepper, to taste
    (optional)

To make the dressing, put the lemon juice and maple syrup in a small bowl and briskly whisk until smooth.

Put the kale, cranberries (or cherries), and walnuts in a large bowl. Pour about three-quarters of the dressing over the salad and toss gently until the kale, cranberries (or cherries), and walnuts are evenly coated. Taste and add the remaining dressing, if desired.

Cover and let stand at room temperature for about 20 minutes before serving. Just before serving, top with a few grinds of sea salt and pepper, if desired.

CHEF'S NOTE

This salad can be made several hours in advance. If you will not be serving it within 20 minutes of preparation, cover and refrigerate it for up to 4 hours.

Fancy Chickpea Salad

[MAKES 2 TO 3 SERVINGS] Reminiscent of chicken salad, this delightful chickpea dish stands in perfectly as a vegan version of a much-loved classic. You may be surprised at how much this salad resembles the real thing!

1 can (15 ounces) chickpeas (garbanzo beans), drained and rinsed

1 cup minced celery with tops (about 2 medium celery stalks)

1½ tablespoons chopped fresh flat-leaf parsley

⅛ teaspoon sea salt

⅛ teaspoon cayenne pepper

1 tablespoon capers, drained, rinsed, and minced

½ cup chopped walnuts

3 to 4 tablespoons vegan mayonnaise or plain vegan yogurt, plus more as needed

Put the chickpeas in a medium bowl and mash them using a potato masher or a large fork. Add the celery, parsley, sea salt, and cayenne pepper and continue mashing to combine. Stir in the capers and walnuts. Stir in the vegan mayonnaise or vegan yogurt, 1 tablespoon at a time, to achieve the desired consistency.

Refrigerate for 2 to 6 hours. Enjoy as a sandwich spread, or serve on a bed of greens for a delicious main-dish luncheon salad.

Kale and Tomato Salad

[MAKES 2 TO 3 SERVINGS] [NUT FREE, NO OIL] A simple-to-prepare kale salad can enhance any meal with its interesting texture and pleasing taste. Paired here with juicy tomatoes, this perfect combo makes a tempting salad almost any time of year.

DRESSING
1 tablespoon Dijon mustard
1 tablespoon maple syrup
1 teaspoon balsamic vinegar
1 clove garlic, minced

SALAD
3 cups very thinly sliced, well packed kale, washed and dried
10 grape tomatoes, halved
¼ teaspoon sea salt
Freshly ground pepper, to taste

Put the Dijon, maple syrup, and balsamic vinegar in a blender and process until thick and smooth. Pour the mustard mixture into a small bowl. Add the garlic and whisk until well-combined.

Put the kale in a large mixing bowl. Pour the dressing over the kale and toss to coat. Leave the kale and dressing to stand at room temperature for 20 to 30 minutes. Right before serving, add the tomatoes and salt. Add pepper to taste. Toss the salad and serve!

Apple, Walnut, and Cinnamon Salad (Anita's Charoset)

[MAKES 3 TO 4 SERVINGS] This traditional Passover salad has a little jazzy twist added, which is the use of organic red grape juice instead of wine. This combo of apple and walnuts, spiced up with a bit of cinnamon, is wonderful to serve any time of year!

1 large or 2 small apples, peeled and chopped
½ cup chopped walnuts
1 tablespoon maple sugar
½ teaspoon ground cinnamon
¼ cup organic red grape juice

Put the apples, walnuts, maple sugar, and cinnamon in a medium bowl and stir to combine. Gently stir in the grape juice. Cover and refrigerate. Serve well chilled.

Pretty Purple Coleslaw

[MAKES 4 SERVINGS] Purple cabbage provides a beautiful color to this twist on a traditional favorite. If you prefer, you can substitute green cabbage and it is still delish!

4 cups grated purple cabbage
(about ½ medium head)
1 cup grated carrots
3 heaping tablespoons vegan mayonnaise
1 tablespoon prepared Dijon mustard
2 teaspoons brown sugar or maple sugar
⅛ teaspoon sea salt
Freshly ground pepper, to taste
1 teaspoon *gomasio*, for garnish (optional)

Put the cabbage, carrots, vegan mayonnaise, Dijon, sugar, and salt in a medium bowl and stir to combine. Season with pepper. Cover and refrigerate 2 to 4 hours. Before serving, sprinkle the top of the salad with *gomasio*, if using.

— CHEF'S NOTE —

[NUT FREE] For a completely nut-free recipe, eliminate optional *gomasio*.

Carrot and Maple Walnut Salad

[MAKES 3 TO 4 SERVINGS] There are just five ingredients in this delightful salad, making it quick to prep but totally delicious to eat! This makes a great choice for a kid's lunchbox or any portable meal.

1¼ cups grated carrots
½ cup chopped walnuts
⅓ cup raisins
2 tablespoons maple syrup
¼ teaspoon sea salt

Put all of the ingredients in a medium bowl and stir gently until well combined. Refrigerate 2 to 4 hours. Serve chilled.

Avocado and Tofu Salad

[MAKES 4 SERVINGS] This is a nice way to showcase tofu. Combined with crunchy almonds, delicate greens, and avocado slices, it makes an appealing first course or main dish salad.

5 cups baby spring greens
6 to 8 ounces firm or extra-firm
    regular tofu, drained and cubed
    (sprouted variety is preferable)
½ large avocado, peeled and thinly
    sliced (see note, page 109)
4 tablespoons raw or roasted almonds
4 tablespoons Lively Lemon Salad
    Dressing (page 53)

Divide the greens among 4 salad plates. For each serving, top with one-quarter of the tofu cubes and avocado slices and 1 tablespoon almonds. Drizzle 1 tablespoon of the dressing over each salad. Serve immediately.

Carrot and Maple Walnut Salad

Deli-Style Macaroni Salad (opposite) with
Italian-Style Sweet Peppers with Vegan Sausage (page 175)

Deli-Style Macaroni Salad

[MAKES 8 TO 10 SERVINGS] [NUT FREE] This classic salad is reminiscent of the kind you'd find in a New York deli. With its traditional taste and delightful texture, it makes an attractive pairing to any picnic or barbecue-style summer meal.

---

1 pound macaroni (see note)
½ cup grated carrots
    (about 1 medium carrot)
½ cup thinly sliced celery
    (about 2 stalks celery)
½ cup sliced black olives (optional)
½ cup vegan mayonnaise, plus more
    as needed
1 tablespoon Dijon mustard, plus
    more as needed
1 tablespoon maple syrup or
    maple sugar
2 to 3 tablespoons minced red or
    yellow onion (about ¼ medium
    onion)
1 teaspoon Italian seasoning
½ cup chopped fresh flat-leaf parsley
¼ teaspoon sea salt, plus more
    as needed
Freshly ground pepper, to taste
½ teaspoon paprika
Tomato wedges, for garnish
    (optional)
Parsley sprigs, for garnish
    (optional)

Bring a large pot of salted water to a boil over medium-high heat. Pour in the macaroni and cook, stirring occasionally, until tender but firm. Drain the macaroni thoroughly, transfer to a large bowl, and let cool until slightly warm. Add the carrots, celery, and olives (if using), and stir gently until well combined.

Put the vegan mayonnaise, Dijon, maple syrup or maple sugar, onion, and Italian seasoning in a small bowl and whisk to combine. Add to the macaroni mixture and stir gently until well combined. Add the parsley, more salt, and pepper to taste, and stir gently until evenly distributed. If a creamier consistency is desired, add more vegan mayonnaise and/or Dijon to taste.

Cover and refrigerate for 2 to 12 hours. Check the consistency before serving; if the mixture seems dry, stir in a bit more vegan mayonnaise, 1 tablespoon at a time. To serve, sprinkle paprika over the top. Garnish with tomato wedges and parsley sprigs, if desired.

CHEF'S NOTE

For a gluten-free option, use your favorite gluten-free pasta in this recipe.

Summer Cucumber Salad

[MAKES 2 SERVINGS] [NUT FREE, NO OIL] This warm-weather staple is inspired by my grandma's recipe. A few seasonal fresh ingredients paired with a pop of vinegar and touch of maple syrup make for a truly refreshing side-dish salad.

1 large cucumber, peeled and
    thinly sliced
½ large sweet or red onion, thinly
    sliced
1 tablespoon balsamic vinegar
1 tablespoon maple syrup
¼ teaspoon paprika, plus more
    for garnish
Sea salt, to taste
Freshly ground pepper, to taste

Put the cucumber and onion in a medium bowl. To make the dressing, put the balsamic vinegar, maple syrup, and paprika in a small bowl and briskly whisk until smooth. Pour the dressing over the cucumbers and onions and toss to coat. Season with sea salt and pepper. Cover and refrigerate for 1 to 6 hours. Sprinkle with additional paprika to garnish, if desired, and serve chilled.

Marinated Asparagus Salad

[MAKES 4 SERVINGS] [NUT FREE, NO OIL] Asparagus makes a refreshing summer salad, adding color and crunch to any meal. It makes a nice light lunch perched on top of a bed of lettuce, or presents an enticing first course to an elegant party meal.

1 tablespoon freshly squeezed
    lemon juice
½ tablespoon reduced-sodium
    tamari
1 clove garlic, minced
1 bunch asparagus, cleaned and
    trimmed

To make the dressing, put the lemon juice, tamari, and garlic in a small bowl and briskly whisk until smooth.

Steam the asparagus until crisp-tender. Put the hot asparagus in a large bowl and add the dressing. Toss gently to coat the asparagus with the dressing. Cover and refrigerate for 3 to 24 hours. Serve chilled on a pretty platter or arranged over a bed of baby greens.

Penne and Black Bean Salad

[MAKES 8 TO 10 SERVINGS] [NUT FREE] Perfect to serve all summer long, this filling and flavorful salad provides a pleasing combination of vibrant color and subtle crunch.

SALAD
1 pound whole-grain penne, cooked al dente and drained
1 can (15 ounces) black beans, drained and rinsed
5 carrots, chopped
1 sweet red pepper, chopped
1 sweet orange or yellow pepper, chopped
1 small sweet onion, diced
1 can marinated artichoke hearts, drained and chopped
12 to 14 leaves chopped fresh basil
4 to 5 leaves chopped fresh oregano
4 leaves chopped fresh sage
2 tablespoons chopped fresh flat-leaf parsley

DRESSING
⅓ cup vegan mayonnaise, plus more as needed (see note)
¼ cup Dijon mustard, plus more as needed
1 heaping tablespoon brown sugar or maple sugar
1 teaspoon Italian seasoning
½ teaspoon turmeric
½ teaspoon sea salt
⅛ teaspoon freshly ground pepper

Put all of the salad ingredients in a very large bowl.

Put all of the dressing ingredients in a blender and process until smooth. Add the dressing to the pasta salad and toss gently until well combined. If a creamier consistency is desired, add more vegan mayonnaise and/or Dijon to taste.

Cover and refrigerate for 3 hours or more until the salad is thoroughly chilled. Serve chilled over a bed of crisp greens with crusty whole-grain bread or rolls on the side.

CHEF'S NOTE

You may use plain vegan yogurt in place of the vegan mayonnaise in this recipe. This substitution works in all of the recipes in this book.

Red Quinoa, Avocado, and Chickpea Salad

[MAKES 4 TO 6 SERVINGS] [NUT FREE] Red quinoa is becoming more commonly available in supermarkets. Here, it adds gorgeous color along with a slightly nutty taste to this hearty main-dish salad.

¾ cup red quinoa, rinsed very well (see note)

1½ cups filtered or spring water

1 can (15 ounces) chickpeas (garbanzo beans), drained and rinsed

2 tablespoons extra-virgin olive oil

4 tablespoons freshly squeezed lemon juice

1 small red onion, diced

1 large clove garlic, minced

1 teaspoon Italian seasoning

¼ teaspoon sea salt, plus more as needed

⅛ teaspoon cayenne pepper

⅛ teaspoon freshly ground pepper, plus more as needed

1 cup chopped fresh flat-leaf parsley

½ cup sweet red pepper, diced

2 medium avocados

CHEF'S NOTE

White quinoa may be used in this recipe.

Put the quinoa and water in a medium sauce pan and bring to a boil over medium heat. Decrease the heat to medium-low, cover, and simmer for 15 to 18 minutes until all of the liquid is absorbed and the quinoa is soft.

Meanwhile, place the chickpeas, 1 tablespoon olive oil, 1 tablespoon lemon juice, onion, garlic, Italian seasoning, salt, cayenne pepper, and pepper in a large mixing bowl. Let the bean mixture stand at room temperature for about 20 minutes.

Put the cooked quinoa in a medium bowl. Toss with 1 tablespoon lemon juice and 1 tablespoon olive oil while it is still warm. Let the quinoa mixture cool for about 15 minutes.

Add the quinoa to the chickpea mixture. Add the parsley, red pepper, and remaining lemon juice. Stir gently to combine. Cover and refrigerate for 2 hours.

Right before serving, cube the avocados and add them to the salad. Toss gently to combine. Serve over lettuce leaves with whole-grain bread on the side. Season with additional salt and pepper to taste.

Quinoa Tabbouleh

[MAKES 4 TO 6 SERVINGS] [NUT FREE] One day I had a bunch of fresh parsley that inspired me to make tabbouleh. I did not have bulgur wheat on hand, but I did have quinoa, which works great in this jazzy twist on a tasty salad.

SALAD
1½ cups cooked quinoa, chilled (see note)
2 tablespoons chopped fresh mint, or 2 teaspoons dried
1 cup chopped fresh flat-leaf parsley
1 tablespoon chopped chives or scallions
½ cup kalamata olives, pitted and sliced
3 medium tomatoes, chopped (about 2½ cups)

DRESSING
2 tablespoons extra-virgin olive oil
1½ teaspoons lemon zest (zest of about ½ medium lemon)
¼ cup freshly squeezed lemon juice
¼ teaspoon sea salt
¼ teaspoon freshly ground pepper
⅛ teaspoon cayenne pepper

Put all of the salad ingredients in a large bowl. Stir to combine. Put all of the dressing ingredients in a medium bowl and whisk together until emulsified. Pour the dressing over the salad and toss to combine. Cover and refrigerate for 2 hours or more before serving. Serve chilled.

CHEF'S NOTE

½ cup of dry quinoa cooked in 1 cup of water or vegetable broth will yield 1½ to 1¾ cups of cooked quinoa.

To cook the quinoa, thoroughly rinse and drain ½ cup of quinoa. Put the quinoa and 1 cup of water in a medium sauce pan and bring to a boil over medium heat. Decrease the heat to medium-low, cover, and simmer for 15 to 17 minutes, until all of the liquid is absorbed and the quinoa is soft. Fluff with a fork. Chill the quinoa for at least 2 hours, or overnight, before using in this salad.

Chickpea and Quinoa Salad in Sweet Pepper Boats

[MAKES 8 SERVINGS] [NUT FREE] These appealing pepper "boats" are filling enough to serve as a main dish for any festive summer meal. Perfectly portable, too, they make a wonderful picnic entrée.

---

1 cup quinoa, rinsed thoroughly and drained

2 cups filtered or spring water

1 can (15 ounces) chickpeas (garbanzo beans), drained and rinsed

½ cup chopped fresh flat-leaf parsley

1 pint grape or cherry tomatoes, halved

¾ cup kalamata olives, pitted and sliced

1 teaspoon lemon zest

2 tablespoons freshly squeezed lemon juice

1 tablespoon extra-virgin olive oil, plus more as needed

1 clove garlic, minced

½ teaspoon chili powder, plus more as needed

¼ teaspoon sea salt, plus more as needed

¼ teaspoon turmeric

4 large sweet red, yellow, or orange peppers

Chopped fresh flat-leaf parsley, for garnish (optional)

Put the quinoa and water in a medium sauce pan and bring to a boil over medium heat. Decrease the heat to medium-low, cover, and simmer for 15 to 17 minutes, until all of the liquid is absorbed. Fluff with a fork. Transfer to a medium bowl. Let cool (see note).

Put the cooled quinoa, chickpeas, parsley, tomatoes, and olives in a large bowl. Put the lemon zest, lemon juice, olive oil, garlic, chili powder, salt, and turmeric in a small bowl and whisk briskly until smooth. Pour the dressing over the quinoa mixture and stir gently to incorporate. Taste and add more chili powder, salt, and/or olive oil if needed. Cover and refrigerate for 2 hours to let the flavors blend. Right before serving, split the peppers in half lengthwise and seed them. Scoop the quinoa mixture into the pepper halves. Garnish with parsley, if using.

CHEF'S NOTE

The quinoa may be cooked up to 24 hours in advance and stored in the refrigerator.

Jazzy Pizza Tart (page 160)

Chapter 9
Pastas and Pizzas with Pizzazz

Any night of the week is the perfect
time to serve a piping hot bowl of pasta or
crowd-pleasing pizza. In this chapter I'll
share my scrumptious vegan versions of
traditional pasta and pizza recipes, plus I've
added a few surprise twists! You can serve
these inspired pastalicious recipes for lunch,
brunch, supper, party, or anytime! It's time
for pasta and pizza with *jazzy pizzazz!*

"Blues is to jazz what yeast is
to bread—without it, it's flat."
—Carmen McRae

Tortilla Salad Pizza

[MAKES 2 SERVINGS] I like to serve this light pizza for a quick-to-make lunch treat. The crust is simply a whole-grain tortilla, making a crisp base for novel toppings.

2 8- to 9-inch whole-grain tortillas

½ tablespoon extra-virgin olive oil

⅔ cup cooked white beans (drained and rinsed if canned)

2 cups well-packed spring salad greens, washed and dried

⅛ teaspoon crushed red pepper

2 medium tomatoes, thinly sliced

¼ teaspoon dried basil

¼ teaspoon dried oregano

Sea salt or Himalayan pink salt

½ sweet red or orange pepper

3 tablespoons shredded vegan cheese (optional)

Almond Parmesan (page 57) (optional)

Preheat the oven to 375 degrees F. Line a large, rimmed baking sheet with unbleached parchment paper.

Put a tortilla on a large plate. Brush both sides of the tortilla with a thin layer of olive oil. Repeat with the second tortilla. Put the tortillas on the prepared baking sheet. Put the beans in a medium bowl and lightly mash them using a potato masher or large fork. Spread half of the mashed beans in an even layer on each tortilla, leaving a slight margin around the edge for a "crust."

Chop the spring greens chiffonade-style (see note). Arrange half of the greens on top of each bean layer. Sprinkle the greens with the crushed red pepper. Arrange the tomatoes in a single layer over the greens and sprinkle with the basil, oregano, and salt. Cut the pepper into 6 slices. Arrange 3 slices of the sweet pepper over the tomatoes on each pizza.

Bake for 20 minutes. Remove the pizzas from the oven and top with vegan cheese (if using). Bake for 5 to 10 minutes, or until the vegan cheese is melted. Serve at once with Almond Parmesan on the side, if desired.

CHEF'S NOTE

Chiffonade is a cutting technique in which leafy greens (such as kale, spring greens, and spinach) and large-leaved herbs (like basil and sage) are cut into long, thin strips. To make a chiffonade cut, stack the leaves, roll them up tightly like a cigar. Cut across the rolled leaves with a sharp knife to produce thin strips.

Festive Stuffed Shells

[MAKES 4 TO 6 SERVINGS] [NUT FREE] I love to make this satisfying pasta dish to serve at festive occasions. The potato pulp, baked and then puréed, stands in beautifully for cheese, while the spinach adds substance and visual interest. The lively color combination of this dish makes a lovely presentation.

20 to 22 jumbo pasta shells
3 to 4 large russet potatoes, baked and cooled (page 209) (see note, page 214)
¼ cup unsweetened nondairy milk
½ cup diced yellow or sweet onion
1 teaspoon fresh minced garlic
¼ teaspoon sea salt
2 cups lightly packed baby spinach, finely chopped
1⅓ cups Dad's Marinara (page 48) or your favorite prepared marinara sauce, plus more for serving
Chopped fresh flat-leaf parsley, for garnish (optional)

CHEF'S NOTES

Serve 3 to 4 shells per person arranged on top of Quick Baby Spinach Salad (page 123).

[NO OIL] For a completely oil-free recipe, use no-oil marinara sauce.

Preheat the oven to 400 degrees F.

Bring a large pot of salted water to a boil over medium-high heat. Add the shells. Decrease the heat to medium-low and cook, stirring occasionally, until the shells are almost cooked but still quite firm. Drain and let cool.

Meanwhile, slice each potato in half lengthwise. Carefully scoop out the pulp, using a teaspoon or grapefruit spoon. Measure out 3 cups of the potato pulp, making sure to pack it very tightly into the measuring cup. Put the 3 cups of the potato pulp in a high-performance blending appliance. Add the nondairy milk, onion, garlic, and salt. Process until smooth. Transfer to a large bowl. Fold the chopped baby spinach into the potato mixture.

Spread 1 cup of the marinara sauce into the bottom of a 9 x 12 inch casserole dish. Spoon about 1½ tablespoons of the potato filling into each of the shells. Place each shell into the prepared casserole dish. Repeat until all shells are stuffed. Top each shell with 1 heaping teaspoon of the marinara sauce. Cover loosely and bake 50 minutes to 1 hour, until the sauce is bubbling. Uncover during the last 5 to 7 minutes of baking for shells to brown slightly. Cool for 5

Festive Stuffed Shells, ready to go into the oven. See final cooked dish on page 39.

to 10 minutes before serving. Sprinkle with optional chopped fresh flat-leaf parsley, if desired. Serve extra sauce in a gravy boat or small bowl to pass around the table.

Spaghetti and Wheatballs

[MAKES 3 TO 4 SERVINGS (12 TO 14 WHEATBALLS)] This dish has an authentic taste and texture, making it a foolproof crowd-pleaser for any family meal. Easy enough to make for a special weeknight meal, but fancy enough to serve when hosting a casual dinner party, this dish will become a staple in your house.

1⅓ cups lightly packed, fresh, soft whole-grain bread crumbs (from about 3 to 4 large slices) (see note)
1 teaspoon Italian seasoning
½ teaspoon garlic powder
⅛ teaspoon sea salt
½ cup chopped walnuts
2 cups chopped mushrooms
½ cup diced onion
¾ pound organic spaghetti (see note)
3 cups prepared vegan marinara sauce, Dad's Marinara (page 48), or your own homemade sauce

CHEF'S NOTES

To make fresh bread crumbs, put 3 to 4 slices of whole-grain bread in a blender and process into coarse crumbs.

The wheatballs make a sensational base for a terrific hero-style sandwich too!

Preheat the oven to 350 degrees F. Line a medium baking pan with unbleached parchment paper.

Put the bread crumbs, Italian seasoning, garlic powder, and salt in a large bowl. Put the walnuts in a blender and pulse to process into coarse crumbs. Add the walnuts to the bread crumbs and stir gently to incorporate.

Put the mushrooms and onion in a blender and process to a chunky purée. Add the mushroom mixture to the walnut/bread crumb mixture and stir to incorporate. Spoon out about 1½ tablespoons of the mushroom mixture and roll it into a ball. Continue in this way with the remaining mushroom mixture. Arrange the rolled wheatballs on the lined baking pan. Bake for 25 to 30 minutes. Gently rotate each wheatball and bake for 12 to 16 minutes more, or until they are crisp and golden.

Bring a large pot of salted water to a boil. Add the spaghetti and cook, stirring occasionally, until tender but firm. Drain the spaghetti well.

Meanwhile, pour the marinara sauce into a medium sauce pan. Bring the sauce to a simmer over medium-low heat. Gently add the wheatballs to the sauce, one at a time, cover, and simmer for 7 to 10 minutes. To

serve, put one-quarter of the spaghetti into each of four pasta bowls, and top with 3 or 4 wheatballs. Ladle marinara sauce over the top and serve immediately.

Pea and White Bean Puttanesca

[MAKES 2 TO 3 SERVINGS] [NUT FREE] Quick to prepare, this zesty pasta dish gets its zing from capers and ease of preparation with the use of frozen peas. You can use any pasta shape that you prefer, but the lasagna noodles give it a fun flair.

3 tablespoons vegetable broth, plus more as needed

1 large scallion, sliced

3 cloves garlic, minced

¼ to ½ teaspoon crushed red pepper

½ teaspoon all-purpose seasoning or Italian seasoning

1½ cups frozen peas

1 cup cooked white beans (drained and rinsed if canned)

2 tablespoons capers, drained and rinsed

1 cup prepared vegan marinara sauce (see note)

8 ounces whole-grain lasagna noodles (broken in half), spaghetti, penne, or fusilli (see note)

Put the broth and scallion in a large skillet. Cook over medium heat for 3 minutes, stirring often. Add the garlic, crushed red pepper, and all-purpose or Italian seasoning, and cook for 2 minutes more, adding more broth, 1 tablespoon at a time, if mixture becomes dry. Add the frozen peas, white beans, capers, and marinara sauce. Decrease the heat to medium-low, cover, and simmer for 15 minutes, or until heated through.

Meanwhile, bring a large pot of salted water to a boil over medium-high heat. Stir in the lasagna noodles. Decrease the heat to medium-low, cover, and cook, stirring occasionally, until tender but firm. Drain the lasagna noodles and add them to the skillet. Toss gently until thoroughly combined. Serve immediately.

CHEF'S NOTES

For a gluten-free option, use your favorite gluten-free pasta in this recipe.

[NO OIL] For a completely oil-free recipe, use no-oil marinara sauce.

Kale-Marinara Sauce with Angel Hair

[MAKES 4 SERVINGS] [NUT FREE] Dr. Pam Popper suggested this innovative way to prepare almighty kale. It is the perfect way to serve a swiftly prepped, budget-conscious, Italian-style meal any night of the week!

1 large bunch kale, cleaned and trimmed, thick stems removed

1 jar (about 25 ounces) low-fat vegan marinara sauce (see note)

1 teaspoon dried basil or 1 tablespoon chopped fresh basil

⅛ to ¼ teaspoon crushed red pepper

2 cloves fresh garlic, chopped

2 tablespoons filtered or spring water, plus more as needed

1 pound whole-grain angel-hair pasta, spaghetti, or your favorite pasta (see note)

Cut the kale into bite-size pieces. Put the kale, marinara sauce, basil, crushed red pepper, garlic, and water in a large skillet. Bring to a simmer, cover, and cook over medium-low heat for 10 to 15 minutes, or until the kale is softened. Add a bit more water, 1 tablespoon at a time, if the mixture becomes dry.

Meanwhile, bring a large pot of salted water to a boil over medium-high heat. Stir in the pasta. Decrease the heat to medium-low and cook, stirring occasionally, until tender but firm. Drain the pasta well. Arrange the pasta on a large platter and pour the sauce over the top. Serve immediately.

CHEF'S NOTES

For a gluten-free option, use your favorite gluten-free pasta in this recipe.

[NO OIL] For a completely oil-free recipe, use no-oil marinara sauce.

Spaghetti with Romaine Lettuce and Olive Sauce

[MAKES 4 SERVINGS] This simple pasta dish features a "no-cook" fresh sauce that prepares in a jiffy. Incorporating crisp romaine lettuce, crunchy walnuts, and tiny tomatoes into this innovative warm-weather pasta dish is incredibly refreshing.

1 pound whole-grain spaghetti, penne, or rigatoni (see note)

1 pint cherry tomatoes, halved

2 to 3 cups, lightly packed, thinly sliced romaine lettuce

12 kalamata olives, pitted and chopped

12 walnuts, chopped

2 tablespoons chopped fresh basil

2 tablespoons chopped fresh flat-leaf parsley

1 teaspoon chopped fresh sage

2 cloves garlic, minced

¼ teaspoon sea salt, plus more as needed

Dash of extra-virgin olive oil (optional)

Freshly ground pepper, to taste

Bring a large pot of salted water to a boil over medium-high heat. Stir in the spaghetti. Decrease the heat to medium-low and cook, stirring occasionally, until tender but firm.

Meanwhile, put the tomatoes in a bowl large enough to also accommodate the spaghetti. With clean hands or the back of a rubber spatula, lightly squeeze the tomatoes to release their juices. Add the lettuce, olives, walnuts, basil, parsley, sage, garlic, and salt. Stir until well combined.

Drain the spaghetti well and, while it is still piping hot, pour it over the tomato mixture. Stir gently until all of the ingredients are thoroughly combined and the lettuce is wilted, adding some olive oil if the mixture seems dry. Season with salt and pepper. Serve immediately.

CHEF'S NOTES

For a gluten-free option, use your favorite gluten-free pasta in this recipe.

Serve with crusty whole-grain or gluten-free rolls for a simple but satisfying summertime meal.

Lemon and Shiitake Mushroom Spaghetti with Capers

[MAKES 4 SERVINGS] [NUT FREE, NO OIL] This light and lively spaghetti dish showcases the meaty taste of shiitake mushrooms. In a pinch you can use cremini mushrooms instead, but the shiitakes add a welcome texture to this delicious dish. Lemon juice provides a delightful dash of fresh flavor.

4 ounces shiitake mushrooms, cleaned, stemmed, and thinly sliced

¼ to ½ cup vegetable broth, plus more as needed

1 teaspoon regular or reduced-sodium tamari

3 tablespoons capers, drained and rinsed

3 cloves garlic, minced

2 tablespoons freshly squeezed lemon juice

1 tablespoon lemon zest (zest of about one large lemon) (optional)

¼ cup chopped fresh arugula

¾ pound whole-grain spaghetti (see note)

CHEF'S NOTE

For a gluten-free option, use your favorite gluten-free pasta in this recipe.

Put the mushrooms and ¼ cup vegetable broth in a large skillet. Cook over medium-low heat for 10 to 12 minutes, stirring occasionally, until the mushrooms are soft. Add a bit more broth, 2 tablespoons at a time, as the mushrooms become dry.

Add the tamari, capers, and garlic. Add more broth, if needed, to keep the mixture from becoming dry. Cover and simmer 5 minutes. Add the lemon juice, lemon zest (if using), and arugula to the sauce. Simmer 5 to 7 minutes more, until the arugula is wilted and heated through, adding a bit of broth, 1 tablespoon at a time, if the sauce becomes dry.

Meanwhile, bring a large pot of salted water to a boil over medium-high heat. Stir in the spaghetti. Decrease the heat to medium-low, cover, and cook, stirring occasionally, until tender but firm. Carefully remove the spaghetti from the pasta pot using a pasta scoop or large tongs, and add it directly into the skillet. Toss gently until thoroughly combined. Serve immediately.

Fresh Tomato and Basil Pie

[MAKES 6 SERVINGS] [NUT FREE] One summer day, I had some exquisite tomatoes that I had purchased at my local farmers' market. I wanted to use them to create a festive and fabulous dish, so I came up with this enticing savory pie.

CRUST
1⅓ cups whole-wheat flour
¼ teaspoon sea salt
⅓ cup extra-virgin olive oil
2 tablespoons cold nondairy milk

TOMATO LAYER
4 large tomatoes, sliced
½ teaspoon Italian seasoning
¼ teaspoon sea salt
2 teaspoons extra-virgin olive oil

BASIL LAYER
½ cup chopped fresh basil
⅓ cup chopped green, black, or
    kalamata olives
5 cremini mushrooms, diced

TOPPING
½ cup shredded vegan cheese
    (optional)

Preheat the oven to 375 degrees F. Oil a 10-inch round pie pan.

To make the crust, put the flour and salt in a medium bowl and stir with a dry whisk to combine. Add the olive oil and stir to combine. Add the nondairy milk, 1 teaspoon at a time, stirring after each addition, to combine. Pull the dough into a ball. Press the dough firmly and evenly into the prepared pie pan, pressing the dough partway up the side of the pan.

Arrange the tomatoes in a spiral design on top of the crust. Sprinkle the tomatoes with the Italian seasoning and salt. Drizzle the olive oil over the entire tomato layer.

Put the basil, olives, and mushrooms in a medium bowl and toss to combine. Top the tomatoes with the basil mixture, spreading it into an even layer.

Bake the pie for 30 minutes. Remove from oven and top with the vegan cheese (if using). Bake for 10 minutes more or until vegan cheese is melted.

Polenta Pizza

[MAKES 4 SERVINGS] [NUT FREE] Polenta as a pizza crust? Yep, it's fabulous! This pizza develops nice crispy edges as it bakes, and the polenta provides a perfect cradle for the fresh tomatoes, artichokes, and fragrant chopped fresh basil leaves. Let's give pizza night a whole new outlook!

CRUST
3 cups plus 2 tablespoons filtered or spring water
1 cup polenta (corn grits)
1 teaspoon dried basil
¼ teaspoon sea salt

TOPPING
2 cloves garlic, minced
¼ teaspoon extra-virgin olive oil (optional)
3 large tomatoes, sliced
4 tablespoons chopped fresh basil
1 teaspoon Italian seasoning
⅛ teaspoon crushed red pepper
Sea salt, to taste
Freshly ground pepper, to taste
5 to 10 marinated artichoke hearts, cut in half

Make the polenta by bringing the water to a boil in a medium sauce pan over medium heat. Decrease the heat to medium-low or low. Pour the polenta steadily into the water, while stirring constantly. Stir in the basil and salt. Stir the polenta frequently for 25 to 30 minutes, or until it is thickened. (The polenta is ready when it easily comes away from the side of the pan and supports a wooden spoon.) Pour the polenta onto a 12-inch pizza pan and carefully spread into an even layer using a rubber spatula. (The edges of the crust should be slightly raised to hold the toppings in place.) Refrigerate for 1 to 2 hours, or until firm to the touch. (The polenta crust may be made the day before, covered, and refrigerated overnight.)

Preheat the oven to 400 degrees F. Bake the crust for 12 minutes. Put the pan on a wire rack and let it stand for 5 to 10 minutes.

Put the garlic and olive oil (if using) in a small bowl and stir to combine. Arrange the tomato slices on top of the crust by overlapping them in a spiral fashion, leaving ¼ inch of the crust exposed on the outer perimeter. Sprinkle the garlic over the tomato slices. Sprinkle 2 tablespoons chopped fresh basil over the tomatoes and garlic. Top

with the Italian seasoning and red pepper. Season with salt and pepper. Arrange the artichokes on top of the pizza. Sprinkle the remaining 2 tablespoons chopped fresh basil over the pizza. Bake for 15 minutes.

Increase the heat to 425 degrees F and bake for 15 to 25 minutes more, or until the crust is crisp and the tomatoes are bubbling hot. Put the pan on a wire rack and cool for 5 to 10 minutes. Slice and serve hot.

Jazzy Pizza Tart

[MAKES 6 SERVINGS] [NUT FREE] Part pizza and part tart, this dish is entirely jazzylicious! The crust is yeast-free, so it is super quick to make and the toppings provide a significant serving of veggies. Serve it up any time your family craves that authentic pizza taste.

TOPPING

½ medium head broccoli, cut into
    bite-size florets
3½ cups sliced cremini or white
    button mushrooms
1 sweet red or orange pepper,
    seeded and thinly sliced
½ small onion, diced
3 teaspoons Italian seasoning
1 teaspoon tamari
1 small eggplant, very thinly sliced
1 teaspoon extra-virgin olive oil
1½ cups prepared marinara, plus
    more as needed
10 queen olives, sliced (optional)
1 cup shredded vegan cheese,
    melting variety (optional)

CRUST

2½ cups whole-wheat flour, plus
    more as needed
2½ teaspoons baking powder
1 teaspoon Italian seasoning
3 tablespoons wheat germ
¼ teaspoon sea salt
1 tablespoon extra-virgin olive oil
1¼ cups filtered or spring water,
    plus more as needed

Preheat the oven to 400 degrees F. Line two 11 x 17 inch rimmed baking sheets with unbleached parchment paper.

Put the broccoli, mushrooms, sweet pepper, onion, 1 teaspoon Italian seasoning, and tamari in a large bowl, and toss to combine. Spread the broccoli mixture in a single layer on one of the prepared baking sheets. Put the eggplant, olive oil, and 1 teaspoon Italian seasoning in a large bowl and toss gently to coat. Place the eggplant in a single layer on the other prepared baking sheet. Put the 2 sheets of vegetables in the oven and bake for 10 minutes, or until crisp-tender. Remove and cool slightly while preparing the dough.

To make the crust, put the flour, baking powder, 1 teaspoon Italian seasoning, wheat germ, and salt in a large mixing bowl and stir with a dry whisk to combine. Add the olive oil and water, and mix with a spoon until incorporated. If the dough is too wet to form into a ball, add more flour, 1 tablespoon at a time, until the dough holds together easily. If the dough is too dry to form into a ball, add more water, 1 tablespoon at a time, until the dough holds together easily. Form the dough into a ball and knead for 1 minute. (Add a bit more water, 1 teaspoon at a time, if the dough seems too stiff to roll out.)

Lightly dust a wooden board or clean, nonporous work surface. Divide the dough in half and place one-half on the prepared work surface. Roll out the dough into an approximately 6 x 9 inch rectangle. Place the rolled-out dough on a clean, nonstick 11 x 17 inch rimmed baking sheet. Press in an even layer to fill half of the baking sheet, rolling the edges inward to make a crust. Repeat with the remaining dough on the other half of the same baking sheet, pressing the two halves together to form a large pizza crust. Spread 1½ cups of marinara in a thin, even layer over the crust, adding more marinara if needed to cover the entire crust. Arrange the partially roasted vegetables over the sauce. Sprinkle the olives (if using) over the vegetables. Sprinkle 1 teaspoon Italian seasoning over the top. Bake for 20 to 25 minutes, until the crust is just beginning to crisp. Top with the vegan cheese (if using). Bake for an additional 5 to 10 minutes or until the vegetables are soft, the vegan cheese has melted, and the bottom of the crust is crisp and golden. Put the baking sheet on a wire rack and cool for 6 to 8 minutes. Cut into squares and serve warm.

Chickpea and Quinoa Salad in Sweet Pepper Boats (page 143)
Jazzylicious Shish Kebabs (page 176)

Chapter 10

Jazzylicious Main Dishes

Do you ever ponder what to serve
as the superstar of your plant-based meal?
If so, this chapter is for you. Whether you
are looking for easy main-dish options for
casual weeknight suppers, fancy recipes
for family get-togethers, festive dishes for
holiday soirées, or elegant entrées for formal
dinner parties, you'll find many fabulous
main-dish recipes here. Yep, family and
friends will be clamoring for an invitation
to your next dinner party!

"One of the very nicest things about life is the way we must regularly stop whatever it is we are doing and devote our attention to eating."

——Luciano Pavarotti

Cashew and Quinoa Loaf (page 166)

Cashew and Quinoa Loaf

[MAKES 5 TO 6 SERVINGS] I love this loaf! It is the ideal main dish to serve at holiday time, but it's so tasty that I like to prepare it at any time of year. This savory loaf is packed with great flavors, and the presentation is super colorful.

LOAF

1½ cups raw cashews

1 cup packed, fresh whole-grain bread crumbs (about 2 slices; see notes)

1½ cups cooked and cooled quinoa (see notes)

4 tablespoons wheat germ, plus more as needed

1 cup diced onion

1 teaspoon extra-virgin olive oil (optional)

1 teaspoon tamari

2 teaspoons vegetable broth, plus more as needed

1 clove garlic, minced

½ cup unsweetened almond milk, plus more as needed

1 tablespoon lemon zest (zest of about one large lemon)

½ teaspoon dried marjoram

½ teaspoon sea salt

⅛ teaspoon freshly ground pepper

FILLING

½ cup diced onion

1 cup diced sweet red pepper

1 teaspoon extra-virgin olive oil (optional)

2 tablespoons filtered or spring water, or vegetable broth, plus more as needed

⅛ teaspoon sea salt

Several grinds of freshly ground pepper

½ cup shredded vegan cheese (optional)

--- CHEF'S NOTES ---

I like to use sprouted-style bread for the bread crumbs in this recipe.

½ cup of dry quinoa cooked in 1 cup of water or vegetable broth will yield 1½ to 1¾ cups of cooked quinoa.

To cook the quinoa, thoroughly rinse ½ cup quinoa under cold running water. Put the quinoa and 1 cup of vegetable broth in a medium sauce pan. Cover and bring to a boil over medium heat. Decrease the heat to medium-low and simmer for 15 to 17 minutes, until all of the liquid has been absorbed. Cover and refrigerate the quinoa for at least 1 hour. The quinoa may be cooked up to 24 hours in advance before preparing this loaf.

Preheat the oven to 400 degrees F. Line an 8 x 4 inch loaf pan with unbleached parchment paper, allowing a 2- to 3-inch overhang on the two lengthwise sides of the pan.

To make the loaf, put the cashews in a blender and process in pulses until they become coarse crumbs (do not overprocess, or you will end up with cashew butter). Place the cashew crumbs, bread crumbs, quinoa, and wheat germ in a large mixing bowl and gently stir until combined. Put 1 cup onion, olive oil (if using), tamari, and vegetable broth in a medium sauté pan and cook over medium heat for 3 minutes or until the onion is translucent. Add a bit more broth, 1 tablespoon at a time, as the mixture gets dry. Add the garlic and sauté 1 minute more. Add the onion mixture to the cashew mixture and stir together until combined.

In a medium bowl, stir together the almond milk, lemon zest, marjoram, salt, and pepper until combined. Stir the almond milk mixture into the cashew–bread crumb mixture. If the mixture seems dry, add more almond milk, 1 tablespoon at a time, until the mixture is slightly wet but holds together easily. Or, if the mixture seems too wet, add more wheat germ, 1 tablespoon at a time, until the mixture holds together. Set the loaf mixture aside.

For the filling, put ½ cup onion, sweet pepper, olive oil (if using), and water or broth in a medium sauté pan and cook for 3 minutes or until the onion is translucent. Add a bit more water or broth as the mixture gets dry. Season with salt and pepper. Remove from the heat and transfer to a medium bowl. Cool for 10 minutes, then stir in the vegan cheese (if using).

Firmly press half of the loaf mixture into the prepared pan. Top with the filling. Using a rubber spatula, spread the filling over the loaf mixture in an even layer. Top with the remaining loaf mixture, spreading it into an even layer with the spatula.

Fold the excess parchment paper over the top of the loaf and press down. This will keep the loaf moist while baking. Press down again to make the loaf more compact. This will help to hold it together.

Bake for 20 minutes. Remove the loaf from the oven and peel back the parchment paper. Bake for 15 to 20 minutes, or until the loaf is slightly golden, firm to the touch, and heated through. Remove the loaf from the oven and cool for 15 minutes. Turn the loaf onto a serving platter and carefully peel off the parchment paper. Cut the loaf into very thick slices, using a serrated bread knife and wiping the knife clean after cutting each slice. Serve warm. Refrigerate leftovers, tightly covered. Leftover loaf will keep up to 2 days. This loaf makes great sandwiches the next day!

Five-Ingredient Black Bean Casserole

[MAKES 4 TO 6 SERVINGS] [NUT FREE] Five ingredients. One mixing bowl. One oven. Delicious dinner. Enough said!

---

2 cans (15 ounces each) black beans, drained and rinsed
1 cup low-fat marinara sauce, plus more as needed (see note)
1 medium sweet onion, chopped
½ teaspoon garlic powder
2 heaping tablespoons maple syrup

Preheat the oven to 375 degrees F. Put all of the ingredients in a large bowl and stir gently to combine. Pour the mixture into a medium casserole dish. Cover and bake for 50 minutes to 1 hour. Serve with a green salad and crusty whole-grain bread.

CHEF'S NOTE

[NO OIL] For a completely oil-free recipe, use no-oil marinara sauce.

Jazzy Tip: Getting your family to eat leafy greens can be challenging. So when you are making layered casseroles or lasagnas, try swapping out one layer in the casserole with organic baby spinach. No need to chop it up. Just add about 6 ounces of baby spinach into one layer of your casserole, and then continue layering with your other ingredients as usual. (It will look like *a lot* of spinach but it *really* cooks down.) As the casserole bakes, the spinach makes a pretty layer in your dish without adding a "spinachy" taste! Mission accomplished!

Easy Burrito Bake

[MAKES 2 SERVINGS] [NUT FREE] My steam/bake method for cooking these delicious burritos makes them slightly crisp on the outside and super moist on the inside. I have been making this dish for many years and it continues to be a favorite midweek, go-to recipe in my kitchen.

---

2 8- to 11-inch whole-grain tortillas

1 to 1¼ cups cooked pinto beans (depending on the size of your tortillas) (drained and rinsed if canned)

½ cup prepared salsa, plus more as needed

¼ cup shredded vegan cheese

4 cups well-packed mixed spring greens

CHEF'S NOTE

[NO OIL] For a completely oil-free recipe, eliminate the vegan cheese.

Preheat the oven to 400 degrees F. Line a 9 x 12 inch baking dish with unbleached parchment paper, allowing a 7-inch overhang on the two lengthwise sides of the dish.

Put a tortilla on a large dinner plate. On one side of the tortilla, layer half of the beans, 2 heaping tablespoons salsa, half of the vegan cheese, and one-third of the greens. Roll the tortilla tightly around the filling and place it seam-side down on the prepared baking dish. Repeat with the remaining tortilla.

Bring the sides of the parchment paper over the burritos, fold it over, and seal tightly. (This will keep the burritos from drying out as they cook.) Bake 30 to 40 minutes, or until heated through. Remove from oven and let stand 5 minutes before unwrapping the parchment.

To serve, place a burrito on a colorful plate and top with 1 to 2 tablespoons salsa. Serve with the remaining greens served on the side.

Savory Mushroom Stroganoff

[MAKES 4 SERVINGS] [NUT FREE, NO OIL] Yum, yum. Thanks to meaty-tasting portobello mushrooms, this satisfying stroganoff has the rich flavor of the traditional version without all of the extra fat and calories.

1 medium sweet onion, chopped

3 to 4 cups vegetable broth, plus more as needed

8 ounces portobello mushrooms, thinly sliced

1 teaspoon dried basil

1 teaspoon reduced-sodium tamari

Pinch of cayenne pepper

8 ounces cremini or white button mushrooms, sliced

1 tablespoon whole-wheat flour, plus more as needed (see note)

½ cup filtered or spring water, plus more as needed

Sea salt, to taste

Freshly ground pepper, to taste

8 ounces whole-grain rotini, fusilli, or other pasta of your choice, cooked and drained

½ cup chopped fresh flat-leaf parsley, for garnish

Put the onion and 2 tablespoons vegetable broth in a large skillet. Cook over medium-low heat, stirring occasionally, until slightly softened, about 5 minutes. Add more broth, 1 tablespoon at a time, if the onion becomes dry.

Add the portobello mushrooms, basil, tamari, and cayenne pepper, and cook, stirring occasionally, about 5 minutes, adding more broth, 1 tablespoon at a time, as needed to prevent sticking. Add the cremini mushrooms and cook, stirring occasionally, until browned, about 8 minutes. Stir in 1½ cups broth. Cover and simmer, stirring occasionally, for 15 to 20 minutes, adding more broth as needed.

Put the flour and ½ cup water in a blender and process until smooth. Briskly whisk the flour-water mixture into the mushrooms. Cook, stirring constantly, until the liquid has thickened to form a gravy. Season with salt and pepper. Serve immediately over the rotini and garnish with parsley.

CHEF'S NOTE

If the gravy is too thick, thin with additional broth to achieve the desired consistency. If the gravy is too thin, thicken with additional flour to achieve the desired consistency.

Sensational Two-Bean Enchilada Casserole

[MAKES 8 TO 10 SERVINGS] [NUT FREE] Whole-grain tortillas, white beans, and tofu provide a fabulous Tex-Mex flair to this impressive casserole. As standalones, the ingredients do not sound exciting, but combined in proper order in this dazzling dish, they create a casserole worth singing about.

---

1 jar (10 to 14 ounces) prepared salsa, plus more as needed

2 teaspoons extra-virgin olive oil (optional)

7 to 10 whole-grain tortillas

1 can (15 ounces) white beans, drained and rinsed

1½ teaspoons tamari

¼ teaspoon cayenne pepper

14 to 16 ounces firm regular tofu, drained

½ teaspoon chili powder

½ teaspoon dried cilantro

1 can (15 ounces) black beans, drained and rinsed

3 cups well-packed baby spinach

1 cup shredded vegan cheese (melting variety)

CHEF'S NOTE

Try using flavored tortillas like habanero or spinach. Be sure to cut the tortillas to fit each layer snugly.

Preheat the oven to 375 degrees F. Spread 2 tablespoons salsa and 1 teaspoon olive oil (if using) evenly in the bottom of a 9 x 12 inch casserole dish. Arrange one layer of the tortillas over the salsa, cutting and trimming the tortillas as you go so they fit snugly into the casserole dish in an even layer.

Put the white beans, ½ teaspoon tamari, and ⅛ teaspoon cayenne pepper in a medium bowl. Mash with a potato masher or large fork until combined. Spread the white bean mixture in an even layer over the tortilla layer in the casserole. Top with 2 to 3 tablespoons salsa, spread in a very thin, even layer.

Arrange another layer of tortillas over the salsa, cutting and trimming the tortillas as needed to create a second even, fitted layer.

Put the tofu, ½ teaspoon tamari, ⅛ teaspoon cayenne pepper, chili powder, and the cilantro in a medium bowl. Mash with a potato masher or large fork until crumbly in texture. Spread the tofu mixture in an even layer over the tortilla layer. Top with ½ to ⅔ cup salsa and spread evenly over the tofu layer. Arrange another

single, even, fitted layer of tortillas over the salsa.

Put the black beans, ½ teaspoon tamari, 1 teaspoon olive oil (if using), and 2 tablespoons salsa in a medium mixing bowl. Mash with a potato masher or large fork until combined. Spread the black bean mixture in an even layer over the tortilla layer.

Add another even, fitted layer of tortillas over the black beans. Top the tortilla layer with the baby spinach and press down gently to compress it. Top the spinach with another ¼ to ⅓ cup salsa, spread in dollops over the spinach.

Add the final layer of tortillas over the salsa, cutting and trimming the tortillas to size as with previous layers. Top with another ¼ cup salsa and spread it evenly over the top. Tent the casserole with foil. Bake for 50 minutes.

Remove the casserole from the oven and remove the foil. Sprinkle the top of the casserole evenly with the vegan cheese. Bake, uncovered, for 15 minutes more, or until the casserole is heated through, bubbling, and the edges are slightly crisp and golden.

Oven-Baked Two-Bean Chili

[MAKES 4 SERVINGS] [NUT FREE, NO OIL] Baking this chili in the oven makes it super simple to feed a crowd. This recipe is easily doubled or tripled if your get-together is super-sized.

CHILI

1 can (15 ounces) black beans, drained and rinsed

1 can (15 ounces) garbanzo beans (chickpeas), drained and rinsed

2 medium sweet onions, chopped

½ teaspoon chili powder

¼ teaspoon garlic powder

⅛ teaspoon cayenne pepper

1 heaping tablespoon unsulphured blackstrap molasses, plus more as needed

⅓ cup organic catsup, plus more as needed

¼ teaspoon sea salt

TOPPINGS

½ cup Vegan Sour "Cream" (page 55) (optional)

¼ cup sliced scallions

½ teaspoon chili powder (optional)

Preheat the oven to 375 degrees F. Put all of the chili ingredients in a large bowl and stir to combine. Pour the mixture into a medium casserole dish. Cover and bake for 35 minutes. Remove the chili from the oven and stir it. If the chili seems dry, add more molasses or catsup to achieve the desired consistency.

Cover and bake for 10 to 20 minutes more, or until bubbling and browned around the edges. Transfer the pan to a wire rack and let cool for 10 minutes before serving. Serve the chili in deep bowls, topped with Vegan Sour "Cream" (page 55) (if using) and scallions. Dust with chili powder (if using).

Italian-Style Sweet Peppers with Vegan Sausage

[MAKES 4 SERVINGS] [NUT FREE] This tantalizing recipe was inspired by the sausage and peppers dish served each year at the annual Feast of San Gennaro in lower Manhattan's Little Italy. With its authentic Italian-American taste and colorful presentation, this is a true crowd-pleaser to serve at any family lunch or casual supper.

1 large sweet onion, thinly sliced
1½ cups vegetable broth, plus more as needed
1 teaspoon Italian seasoning
1/16 to 1/8 teaspoon cayenne pepper
3 sweet yellow, red, and/or orange peppers, cored and sliced
4 large (14 to 16 ounces) vegan sausages

Put the onion and 2 tablespoons broth in a large skillet. Cook over medium-low heat for 3 minutes. Add the Italian seasoning and cayenne pepper. Cover and cook for 3 minutes. Add more broth, 1 tablespoon at a time, as needed to prevent sticking. Add the peppers. Cover and cook, stirring occasionally, for 5 minutes, adding more broth, 1 tablespoon at a time, as needed to prevent sticking.

Slice each sausage, on the diagonal, into 5 or 6 pieces. Add the sausage and the remaining broth to the skillet. Cover and cook 6 to 7 minutes, adding more broth, 1 tablespoon at a time, as needed to prevent sticking.

Serve immediately in warm, crusty, hoagie-style buns or spooned over brown rice, quinoa, or whole-grain pasta.

Jazzylicious Shish Kebabs

[MAKES 5 TO 6 SERVINGS] [NUT FREE, NO OIL] These jazzy shish kebabs will satisfy vegans and meat-eaters alike. The colorful and impressive presentation is sure to add a festive touch to your barbecue meal. To make it super easy, you can use your favorite bottled vegan barbecue sauce or whip up my tasty Zesty BBQ Sauce (page 43).

Zesty BBQ Sauce (page 43)
2 packages cubed seitan, well drained (see note)
3 sweet peppers (orange, red, and/or yellow), seeded and cut in 1½-inch pieces
2 medium sweet onions, cut into chunks
2 medium zucchini, cut into ½-inch thick slices
16 ounces cremini mushrooms, cleaned and stems removed
20 cherry tomatoes
10 to 12 metal or bamboo skewers

Cover two large, rimmed baking sheets with foil or unbleached parchment paper.

Prepare barbecue sauce, and set aside.

Put the seitan in a large bowl and top it with ¼ cup of the sauce. Gently toss the seitan to coat. Cover and refrigerate for 1 to 2 hours to marry the flavors.

Put the peppers, sweet onions, zucchini, mushrooms, and tomatoes in a large bowl. Top with ¾ cup of the sauce (leaving about ½ cup in reserve) and toss to coat. Cover and refrigerate 1 to 2 hours to marry the flavors. Prepare

CHEF'S NOTES

You may use about 1½ blocks (16 to 20 ounces) extra-firm tofu, drained and pressed, instead of the seitan. It is necessary to use extra-firm tofu for the shish kebab. Medium or soft tofu will break apart while cooking. In addition, it is important to drain the tofu well, so it will properly absorb the barbecue sauce.

To drain and press tofu, start by placing a large colander in your sink. Put the block of tofu in the colander. Press down on the tofu lightly with your hands to release excess water. Put a medium-size plate on top of the tofu. Put an unopened can of soup or beans on top of the plate to weigh the plate down.

Allow the tofu to drain for 15 to 30 minutes. This will remove a good deal of water from the tofu. Remove the can and the plate, and your tofu is ready to use.

two metal or bamboo skewers for each person. If you are using bamboo skewers, place them in a pan and cover them with filtered or spring water. Let the skewers soak in the water for about 30 minutes prior to assembling the kebabs to prevent them from burning.

To assemble the kebabs, carefully thread the kebab ingredients onto your prepared skewers in the following order:

> Pepper
> Seitan
> Zucchini
> Mushroom
> Onion
> Pepper
> Seitan
> Tomato
> Onion
> Zucchini
> Seitan
> Mushroom
> Tomato
> Pepper

Arrange the kebabs evenly on the prepared baking sheets. (If you are not baking or grilling them immediately,

cover loosely with foil, and place the sheets back in the refrigerator for up to 2 hours before cooking.)

If grilling:

Place the kebabs directly on the grill. Grill the kebabs over medium heat for about 20 minutes or until the veggies are crisp-tender and the seitan is slightly crisp and golden in color. While the kebabs are grilling, rotate them often, frequently brushing them with additional barbecue sauce to keep them moist.

If baking:

Preheat the oven to 400 degrees F. Leave the kebabs on the baking sheets. Bake for 20 minutes. Rotate the kebabs once, and brush them with additional barbecue sauce. If the kebabs are browning too quickly, loosely tent the baking sheets with foil. Continue baking for 20 minutes or until the veggies are crisp-tender and the seitan is slightly crisp and golden in color.

Serve shish kebabs over Quick Quinoa (page 219) or brown rice to add an extra pop of texture and flavor.

Walnut-Stuffed Portobello Mushrooms

[MAKES 5 TO 6 SERVINGS] Yum is all I can say! I have served these beauties on many festive occasions to rave reviews from all diners at the table. They look lovely when served on a bed of steamed or sautéed greens. Here's a jazzy bonus: they are really easy to prepare!

6 medium portobello mushrooms, stemmed
3 teaspoons tamari
4 slices whole-grain bread
1 cup chopped walnuts
2 teaspoons Italian seasoning
2 teaspoons dried basil or 2 tablespoons chopped fresh basil
2 teaspoons extra-virgin olive oil, plus more as needed
½ teaspoon garlic powder

Preheat the oven to 375 degrees F. Line a large, rimmed baking sheet with unbleached parchment paper.

Briefly rinse the portobello mushrooms and pat dry with a clean dish towel, taking care not to break them. Put the mushrooms upside-down on the prepared baking sheet, and drizzle each mushroom with ½ teaspoon tamari.

Put the bread, walnuts, Italian seasoning, basil, olive oil, and garlic powder in a high-performance blending appliance. Process until the mixture resembles coarse crumbs. Fill each mushroom with one-sixth of the walnut mixture, patting it down firmly.

Tent the mushrooms with foil and bake for 30 minutes. Remove the foil and bake for 10 minutes longer, until the topping is crisp and the mushrooms are tender. Serve immediately.

Easy Vegan Paella

[MAKES 5 TO 6 SERVINGS] [NUT FREE] For years, my husband asked me to come up with a vegan version of paella. One day, he bought me a paella pan and I was immediately inspired to create this delicious one-pot meal. If you don't have a paella pan, don't let that stop you. A large, thick-bottomed pan will do nicely, so I heartily suggest giving this enticing recipe a try!

1 can (28 ounces) whole peeled tomatoes, with liquid

8 to 10 ounces cremini mushrooms, cleaned and stemmed

2 cups long-grain brown rice or brown basmati rice (see note)

2 cloves garlic, minced

1 sweet red pepper, diced

1 cup frozen peas

4 scallions, sliced

½ cup chopped fresh flat-leaf parsley

1¾ cups vegetable broth, plus more as needed

½ teaspoon paprika

½ teaspoon turmeric

¼ teaspoon sea salt

1 jar (12 ounces) artichoke hearts, packed in oil, partially drained

──── CHEF'S NOTE ────

Basmati rice works best in this recipe.

Put the tomatoes and their juice in a medium bowl and break up slightly using a potato masher or large fork. Put the crushed tomatoes, mushrooms, rice, garlic, red pepper, frozen peas, scallions, parsley, vegetable broth, paprika, turmeric, and salt in a very large mixing bowl and stir well to combine. Pour the mixture into a large skillet or paella pan that has a tight-fitting lid.

Cover and cook over medium-low heat for about 50 minutes. Remove cover. Gently stir the paella. Press the artichokes one by one into the top of the paella, arranging them evenly over the top of the rice. If the paella seems dry at this point, pour ¼ to ½ cup more broth over top of the paella. Do not stir!

Cover and cook 15 to 25 minutes or until the liquid is absorbed and the rice is soft, checking occasionally. If the rice is still firm, add ¼ cup more vegetable broth and cook for 10 to 15 minutes more. Serve in pretty bowls with whole-grain bread on the side.

Coconut-Encrusted Tofu Cutlets

[MAKES 3 TO 4 SERVINGS] Coconut and wheat germ provide a luscious crunchy coating that encases delicately flavored tofu "cutlets." If you have had a difficult time getting your family to eat tofu, here is the perfect dish to try. It's tofulicious!

---

14 to 16 ounces extra-firm regular tofu, drained
⅔ cup raw unsweetened shredded dried coconut
⅓ cup wheat germ (see note)
¼ teaspoon turmeric
⅛ teaspoon cayenne pepper
⅓ cup reduced-sodium tamari
Maple-Scallion Dipping Sauce (page 45)

CHEF'S NOTE

You may use oat bran in place of the wheat germ, if desired.

Preheat the oven to 400 degrees F. Line a rimmed baking sheet with unbleached parchment paper.

Cut the tofu into 12 pieces using the following method: Lay the tofu flat on a cutting board, and slice in half. Stand one half on end and slice horizontally into 3 even slices. Stack the slices and cut in half. Repeat with second half of the tofu.

Put the coconut, wheat germ, turmeric, and cayenne pepper in a medium bowl and whisk together to combine. Pour the tamari into a small bowl. Dip each tofu cutlet into the tamari to coat all sides, then immediately dip it into the coconut mixture. Coat the tofu generously with the coconut mixture, patting it down to help it adhere. Put the tofu cutlet on the prepared sheet. Repeat with the remaining tofu pieces until they are all coated.

Tent the baking sheet loosely with foil, being careful not to let the foil touch the tops of the cutlets. Bake for 30 to 35 minutes. Remove foil and bake an additional 5 to 15 minutes, or until the coating is golden brown and crunchy. Serve with Maple-Scallion Dipping Sauce (page 45) on the side.

Mushroom-Nut Burgers

[MAKES 4 SERVINGS] For years I tried and tried to come up with an easy way to make a great-tasting burger substitute. When paired with a whole-grain bun, this burger has a hearty texture and robust taste that stands in magnificently for the meat-based version.

1½ cups lightly packed, fresh, soft whole-grain bread crumbs (from about 3 to 4 large slices) (see notes)

1 teaspoon Italian seasoning or all-purpose seasoning

½ teaspoon chili powder

½ teaspoon garlic powder

⅛ teaspoon sea salt

½ cup chopped walnuts

2 cups chopped mushrooms

⅓ cup diced onion

1 teaspoon reduced-sodium tamari or ¼ teaspoon sea salt

CHEF'S NOTES

For a gluten-free option, make gluten-free bread crumbs using your favorite gluten-free bread in place of the whole-grain bread.

To make fresh bread crumbs, put 3 to 4 large slices of whole-grain bread in a blender and process into coarse crumbs.

Preheat the oven to 375 degrees F. Line a medium baking pan with unbleached parchment paper.

Put the bread crumbs, Italian or all-purpose seasoning, chili powder, garlic powder, and salt in a large bowl. Put the walnuts in a blender and process in pulses until they resemble coarsely ground flour. Add the walnuts to the bread crumbs and stir gently to incorporate. Put the mushrooms, onion, and tamari in a blender and process to a chunky purée. Add the mushroom mixture to the walnut–bread crumb mixture and stir to incorporate.

Place a 3-inch cookie cutter ring on the parchment. Pack one-quarter of the mushroom–bread crumb mixture into the ring and press it firmly and evenly into the ring to form a "burger." Gently remove the ring. Repeat with the remaining mushroom–bread crumb mixture.

Flatten each burger slightly with the back of a flat spatula. Bake for 18 minutes. Flip each burger and bake for an additional 15 to 25 minutes, or until the burgers are slightly crisp and golden.

Serve on toasted whole-grain buns, topped with lettuce, tomato, sweet onion, mustard, and catsup. These burgers are delightful served with Confetti Oven Fries (page 217) and Pretty Purple Coleslaw (page 130) on the side.

Sweet and Sour Stuffed Cabbage

[MAKES 4 TO 6 SERVINGS] Based on my mother-in-law's traditional family recipe, this dish is totally tasty. The freshly squeezed lemon juice balances beautifully with the brown sugar, making a truly sweet and sour sauce for these hearty, savory stuffed cabbage rolls. A fabulous holiday dish or satisfying weeknight meal!

SAUCE

1 cup diced onion

1 cup vegetable broth

1 teaspoon all-purpose seasoning

½ teaspoon reduced-sodium tamari

1 can (28 ounces) whole peeled tomatoes, with liquid, lightly mashed

⅓ cup brown sugar or maple sugar

2 tablespoons freshly squeezed lemon juice

2 cloves garlic, minced

ROLLS

Large head of green cabbage

2 cups cooked brown rice (long-grain or basmati)

¾ cup walnuts

1 slice whole-grain bread

1 teaspoon all-purpose seasoning

¼ teaspoon sea salt

2 cups chopped mushrooms

1 cup diced onion

Preheat the oven to 375 degrees F.

To make the sauce, put 1 cup diced onion, ⅓ cup vegetable broth, all-purpose seasoning, and tamari in a medium sauce pan. Cover and simmer over medium-low heat for 5 minutes. Add the remaining ⅔ cup broth, tomatoes, sugar, lemon juice, and garlic. Cover and simmer for 15 minutes while preparing the cabbage rolls.

Fill a large soup pot two-thirds full with water. Bring to a simmer over medium-high heat.

Meanwhile, remove the core from the cabbage. Gently separate 12 whole leaves from the cabbage (it's fine if they tear a bit). Reserve remaining cabbage for another use.

Remove the pot of simmering water from the heat. Carefully place each cabbage leaf in the pot of water until they are all submerged. Cover and let stand for 4 to 5 minutes to allow the cabbage leaves to soften. Remove the leaves and place them in a large colander to drain and cool.

To make the filling, put the brown rice in a large bowl. Put the walnuts in a blender and pulse to process into coarse crumbs. Add the walnuts to the brown rice. Put the bread, all-purpose seasoning, and salt in a blender and process until

coarsely ground. Add the bread mixture to the brown rice.

Put the mushrooms and 1 cup diced onion in a blender and process into a chunky purée. Add the mushroom mixture to the brown rice. Stir gently to combine all of the filling ingredients.

Spread ¾ cup of the tomato sauce evenly in the bottom of a 9 x 12 inch casserole dish. Lay a cabbage leaf flat on a large dinner plate. If the leaf still has some of the thick stem attached, carefully cut

around it with a small paring knife to remove. This will make the leaves easier to roll up around the filling.

Mound ¼ cup of the filling in the center of the leaf. Fold the sides inward and roll the cabbage leaf firmly around the filling. Place the cabbage roll seam-side down in the prepared casserole. Repeat with the remaining leaves. Pour the remaining sauce over the rolls and cover tightly. Bake for 70 to 90 minutes, or until the cabbage is soft. Cool for 10 to 15 minutes before serving.

Cauliflower Steaks with Sweet Pepper Sauce

[MAKES 6 SERVINGS] [NUT FREE] My husband loves cauliflower. Once, he came home from the market with copious amounts of cauliflower and I knew I needed to come up with a new cauliflower recipe . . . and fast! The result is this colorful, impressive, and satisfying entrée that is ideal to serve throughout the fall and winter seasons.

---

2 medium heads of cauliflower
1 red onion, thinly sliced
1 yellow or sweet onion, thinly sliced
2 teaspoons Italian seasoning
1 teaspoon reduced-sodium tamari
¼ cup filtered or spring water, plus
    more as needed
2 cups cremini or white button
    mushrooms, thinly sliced
2 sweet red peppers, thinly sliced
1 green pepper, thinly sliced
2 cups jarred, low-fat marinara sauce
    or Dad's Marinara (page 48), plus
    more as needed (see note)

CHEF'S NOTE

[NO OIL] For a completely oil-free recipe, use no-oil marinara sauce.

Preheat the oven to 375 degrees F.

Trim one to two inches off two opposite sides of the cauliflower heads, and set aside for another use. Steam the trimmed cauliflower heads for 12 to 18 minutes or until they are just crisp-tender. Cool for 20 minutes.

Meanwhile, put the onion, Italian seasoning, tamari, and 2 tablespoons water in a large skillet. Cover and cook over medium heat for 5 minutes, adding more water, 1 tablespoon at a time, as needed to prevent sticking. Add the mushrooms and cook for 5 minutes. Add the peppers and 2 tablespoons water, and continue to cook for 5 minutes. Decrease the heat to medium-low and stir in 1 cup of the marinara. Cover and simmer for 8 minutes.

Spread 1 cup marinara sauce evenly in the bottom of a rimmed casserole that is large enough to accommodate the cauliflower steaks. Cut each cauliflower head into three ¾-inch to 1-inch thick slices, as if slicing a loaf of bread. Set the cauliflower slices in the prepared casserole and top each with one-sixth of the onion and

pepper sauce. Cover and bake 25 to 35 minutes or until the cauliflower steaks are tender but still firm. Uncover the casserole for the last 10 minutes of cooking time. Cool for 5 minutes. Serve with extra sauce on the side.

Zucchini Summer Quiche

[MAKES 6 SERVINGS] A warm-weather brunch calls for quiche, so I created this vegan version to pleasingly fit the bill. Featuring shredded zucchini and a flaky, gluten-free crust, this quiche will be declared a winner when served at any midday meal.

CRUST
1 cup garbanzo bean (chickpea) flour
3 heaping tablespoons sesame tahini
3 tablespoons cold nondairy milk, plus more as needed

FILLING
2 medium zucchini and/or yellow summer squash
14 to 16 ounces soft or firm regular tofu, drained
1½ teaspoons Italian seasoning
½ teaspoon turmeric
½ teaspoon chili powder
½ teaspoon sea salt
⅛ teaspoon cayenne pepper
½ teaspoon maple syrup
⅓ cup diced sweet red pepper
2 tablespoons minced onion
¾ cup shredded vegan cheese
Freshly ground pepper, to taste
½ to 1 teaspoon regular or smoked paprika
Preheat the oven to 400 degrees F.

Oil a 9-inch pie plate.

To make the crust, put the garbanzo bean flour in a medium bowl. Add the tahini and the cold nondairy milk. Mix together using a pastry cutter or fork until the dough begins to form into chunks the size of large peas. Pull the dough together with your hands. If it is still too crumbly to form into a ball, add more of the cold nondairy milk, 1 tablespoon at a time, up to 3 tablespoons.

Form the dough into a ball and place it in the prepared pie plate. Gently press the dough evenly over the bottom and partway up the sides of the pie plate. Bake the crust for 7 minutes. Put the plate on a wire rack and cool for 20 minutes.

While the crust bakes, cut 10 to 12 very thin slices from the center of one zucchini and set aside for garnish. Using a box grater, shred enough of the remaining zucchini to equal 1½ cups (lightly packed). Put the 1½ cups shredded zucchini in a fine meshed strainer and place it over a medium bowl. Let the shredded zucchini stand for 10 minutes to drain excess liquid.

Meanwhile, put the tofu, Italian seasoning, turmeric, chili powder, salt, and cayenne pepper in a blender and process until smooth.

Before removing the zucchini from the strainer, press it gently with your hands to push out any excess liquid. Put the zucchini and maple syrup in a large bowl and stir gently to coat. Add the red pepper and onion, and stir to combine. Add the tofu to the zucchini mixture. Add the vegan cheese and fresh pepper, and stir gently to combine.

Pour the tofu mixture into the crust. Smooth the top. Cut the reserved zucchini slices in half and press them into the top of the quiche in a decorative fashion. Sprinkle the paprika in an even layer over the top. Bake for 50 to 60 minutes until the center is set. Put the pan on a wire rack and cool for at least 60 minutes before slicing into wedges. May be served warm or refrigerated and served chilled.

Savory Seitan Loaf with Tomato-Mushroom Gravy

[MAKES 6 SERVINGS] [NUT FREE] This savory loaf makes use of seitan, also known as "wheat meat," to give it a hearty flair. Sides of Twice-Baked Potatoes (page 214) and Broccoli with Sweet Tamari-Onion Sauce (page 204) round out this family favorite.

¾ cup minced onion
1 cup minced celery
¼ cup filtered or spring water, plus more as needed
½ teaspoon extra-virgin olive oil (optional)
1 teaspoon reduced-sodium tamari or ¼ teaspoon sea salt
1 tablespoon plus 1 teaspoon Italian seasoning
16 ounces seitan, drained
⅔ cup rolled oats
1 cup grated carrots
½ teaspoon paprika
½ teaspoon garlic powder
½ teaspoon sea salt
5 tablespoons tomato paste
3 tablespoons toasted wheat germ
1 cup baby spinach, finely chopped
Tomato-Mushroom Gravy (page 45)

CHEF'S NOTE

[NO OIL] For a completely oil-free recipe, omit the optional olive oil.

Preheat the oven to 375 degrees F. Line an 8 x 4 inch loaf pan with unbleached parchment paper, allowing a 2- to 3-inch overhang on the two lengthwise sides of the pan.

Put the onion, celery, 2 tablespoons water, olive oil (if using), and tamari in a skillet. Cover and cook over medium heat for 5 minutes. Add 1 teaspoon Italian seasoning and 2 tablespoons water. Cover and cook 5 minutes or until the onion is translucent. Cool for 5 minutes.

Put the seitan in a high-performance blending appliance and process until coarsely ground. Transfer the seitan to a large bowl.

Put the rolled oats, carrots, paprika, garlic powder, remaining 1 tablespoon Italian seasoning, and salt in a large bowl and stir until combined. Add the celery mixture, 3 tablespoons of the tomato paste, and wheat germ, and stir until combined. Fold in the spinach and stir gently until combined.

Spread the remaining 2 tablespoons tomato paste evenly over the parchment paper in the bottom of the prepared loaf pan. Put the seitan mixture on top of the tomato paste layer. Firmly press the seitan mixture into the

pan. Fold the excess parchment paper over the top of the loaf and gently press down. This will keep the loaf moist while baking and help the loaf to hold together.

Bake the loaf for 30 minutes. Remove the loaf from the oven and gently peel back the parchment paper that is covering the top of the loaf. Place the loaf back in the oven for 30 minutes. Loosely tent some foil over the loaf and bake for 15 to 20 minutes, or until the loaf is slightly golden in color and almost firm to the touch. Put the pan on a wire rack and let cool for 5 minutes.

Turn the loaf onto a serving platter and carefully peel off the parchment paper. Cool for 5 to 15 minutes. Cut the loaf into thick slices, using a serrated bread knife and wiping the knife clean after cutting each slice. Serve topped with Tomato-Mushroom Gravy (page 45).

Holiday White Bean, Potato, and Stuffing Casserole

[MAKES 6 SERVINGS] Holidays can be challenging when you are serving vegans and meat-eaters alike. But fret no more! This hearty stuffing-based casserole contains the comfort-food "feel" of shepherd's pie—sans the meat, dairy, and eggs, of course!

POTATO/BEAN LAYER

3 cups peeled and chopped white
    potatoes
1½ cups cooked white beans
    (drained and rinsed if canned)
¼ teaspoon garlic powder
¼ teaspoon sea salt
1 teaspoon dried marjoram leaves

STUFFING

4 cups whole-grain bread cubes,
    from 7 to 9 slices fresh whole-
    grain bread (see note)
3 teaspoons Italian seasoning (see
    note)
½ teaspoon sea salt
2 cups diced onion
2¼ cups vegetable broth
1 teaspoon dried basil
1 cup diced celery
4 cups diced mushrooms
⅔ cup chopped pecans

GARNISH

½ teaspoon paprika, plus more as
    needed

Preheat the oven to 400 degrees F. Oil an 11 x 7 inch baking pan or casserole dish.

To make the potato/bean layer, fit a large sauce pan with a steamer insert. Add 2 inches of cold water, and then add the potatoes. Cover and bring to a boil. Steam for 15 to 20 minutes, until they are soft, but not mushy. Put the potatoes, beans, garlic powder, and salt in a high-performance blending appliance and process until smooth. Transfer to a medium-size bowl and stir in the marjoram.

While the potatoes are steaming, cut the whole-grain bread into 1/2-inch cubes. Put the bread cubes, Italian seasoning, and salt in a large bowl and toss to combine. Transfer to a large, rimmed baking sheet and bake for 10 to 15 minutes or until the bread is slightly crisp. Put the pan on a wire rack and let cool.

While the bread cubes are cooling, prepare the stuffing by combining the onion, ¼ cup vegetable broth, and the basil in a large skillet. Cook over medium-low heat, stirring occasionally, for 7 minutes. Add the celery and ¼ cup broth, cover, and cook, stirring occasionally, for 5 minutes. Add the diced mushrooms and

another ¼ cup broth, cover, and cook, stirring occasionally, for 5 minutes, or until most of the liquid has cooked down, leaving the mushroom mixture very moist but not soupy. Stir in the pecans and remove the skillet from the heat.

Put the remaining 1½ cups vegetable broth into a small sauce pan. Bring to a simmer over medium heat. Put 4 cups of the toasted bread cubes in a large bowl. Add the mushroom-pecan mixture and stir gently to combine. Pour in ½ cup of the hot vegetable broth and stir to

combine. Add as much of the remaining broth as needed so the mixture is moist but not soupy. (If the mixture still seems dry after adding all of the broth, add a small amount of water.)

Spread the stuffing in an even layer in the bottom of the prepared baking pan or casserole dish. Spread the potato mixture over the stuffing in an even layer. Sprinkle with the paprika. Cover loosely and bake for 40 to 45 minutes. Uncover and bake for 5 to 7 minutes, until slightly golden on top. Cool for 15 minutes. Serve warm.

CHEF'S NOTES

For a gluten-free option, make gluten-free stuffing using 7 to 9 slices of gluten-free bread in place of the whole-grain variety.

If you prefer a sage-flavored stuffing, replace the 3 teaspoons Italian seasoning with 1 teaspoon crumbled dried sage leaves, 1 teaspoon dried thyme leaves, and 1 teaspoon dried marjoram leaves.

Maple-Baked Acorn Squash (page 208)

Chapter 11

Symphony of Sides

Side dishes can make a ho-hum menu spectacular. Side dishes add color, texture, flavor, and visual appeal to your meal. Gorgeous grains, green veggies topped with luscious sauces, succulent squashes, and vibrant root vegetables all transform a plain meal into a vegan feast. Whether you serve them roasted, baked, sautéed, mashed, steamed, boiled, or raw, side dishes are the perfect way to jazz up any plant-based meal.

"*A jazz musician is a juggler who uses harmonies instead of oranges.*"

—Benny Green

Kale with Walnut "Cream" Sauce

[MAKES 4 TO 6 SERVINGS] Eat your greens. We've all heard that eating plenty of leafy greens is a healthful addition to any diet. But how do you make greens taste good? Hmm. . . . To tell the truth, I sometimes have trouble convincing my husband to eat greens. So when I first prepared this great all-purpose sauce to dress up veggies, I rejoiced because he *loved* it! Now I pass this super easy recipe on to you!

---

1 large bunch kale, washed and very thinly sliced
½ cup chopped walnuts
½ cup filtered or spring water, plus more as needed
1 teaspoon tamari
½ teaspoon Italian seasoning
1 clove garlic, halved

CHEF'S NOTE

The walnuts will immediately develop a creamy consistency when blended, making this a great substitute for cream-based salad dressings. It also makes a great topper for brown rice, quinoa, pasta, or steamed tofu.

Fit a steamer basket into a large sauce pan with a tight-fitting lid. Add 2 inches of cold water, then add the kale. Cover and bring to a boil. Steam for 10 to 12 minutes, until wilted and quite soft but still bright green. Transfer to a medium bowl.

Meanwhile, put the walnuts, water, tamari, Italian seasoning, and garlic in a blender and process until smooth, adding more water if needed, 2 tablespoons at a time, to achieve the desired consistency.

Pour the sauce over the kale and toss to coat evenly. Serve immediately.

Asparagus with Vegan Hollandaise Sauce

[MAKES 4 TO 6 SERVINGS] [NUT FREE, NO OIL] Asparagus is one of the first crops of spring. Paired with rich-tasting vegan "hollandaise" sauce, it makes the perfect vegetable side dish for any special meal! My grandmother grew asparagus in her backyard and she often served it with a rich hollandaise sauce that I, as a child, loved! So, I came up with this easy-to-prepare vegan version that tastes delicious and is low in fat, too!

---

1 large bunch asparagus, trimmed
3 tablespoons fresh lemon juice
8 ounces soft silken or regular tofu, drained
¼ teaspoon turmeric
¼ teaspoon sea salt

Fit a steamer basket into a medium sauce pan with a tight-fitting lid. Add 2 inches of cold water, then add the asparagus. Cover and bring to a boil. Steam the asparagus for 4 to 6 minutes or just until crisp-tender.

Meanwhile, put the lemon juice, tofu, turmeric, and salt in a blender and process until smooth. Transfer to a small sauce pan and cook over low heat, stirring constantly, until heated through.

Arrange the hot asparagus on a serving platter and pour the sauce over top. Serve immediately.

Broccoli with Lemon Sauce

[MAKES 4 SERVINGS] [NUT FREE] I like to dress up hot, steamed broccoli with the citrusy notes of freshly squeezed lemon juice. Simple, light, and delicious!

1 head broccoli, cut into florets
1 tablespoon extra-virgin olive oil
1 tablespoon freshly squeezed
   lemon juice
¼ teaspoon tamari
⅛ teaspoon garlic powder, plus
   more as needed
Sea salt, to taste
Freshly ground pepper, to taste

Fit a steamer basket into a medium sauce pan with a tight-fitting lid. Add 2 inches of cold water, then add the broccoli. Cover and bring to a boil. Steam for 8 to 10 minutes, until crisp-tender. Transfer to a medium bowl.

Put the olive oil, lemon juice, tamari, and garlic powder in a small bowl and whisk to combine. Pour the sauce over the broccoli and toss until the broccoli is evenly coated. Season with salt and pepper, to taste. Serve immediately.

Petite Peas and Parsnips

[MAKES 4 TO 6 SERVINGS] [NUT FREE] The simple but tantalizing blend of parsnips and peas makes a colorful dish that is full of flavor.

4 parsnips, peeled and thinly sliced
1 bag (16 ounces) frozen organic
   petite peas
2 teaspoons vegan margarine
   (optional)
¼ teaspoon sea salt
Freshly ground pepper, to taste

Fit a steamer basket into a medium sauce pan with a tight-fitting lid. Add 2 inches of cold water, then add the parsnips. Cover and bring to a boil. Steam for 6 to 8 minutes, or until crisp-tender. Add the frozen peas. Continue to steam until the peas are hot and the parsnips are soft, about 3 minutes more. Transfer to a large bowl. Add the vegan margarine (if using), salt, and pepper to taste. Toss gently until the parsnips and peas are evenly coated. Serve warm.

Broccoli with Sweet Tamari-Onion Sauce

[MAKES 4 SERVINGS] [NUT FREE, NO OIL] This simple combo is a fancy and flavorful way to serve broccoli. Serve this dish on the side to add a refreshing pop-of-green to just about any entrée.

1 large head broccoli, washed and
    cut into bite-size florets
1 tablespoon tamari
1 tablespoon maple sugar
1 tablespoon minced onion
1 large clove garlic, minced

Fit a steamer basket into a medium sauce pan with a tight-fitting lid. Add 2 inches of cold water, then add the broccoli. Cover and bring to a boil. Steam for 8 to 10 minutes until crisp-tender. Transfer to a medium bowl.

Meanwhile, put the tamari, maple sugar, onion, and garlic in a small bowl and whisk to combine. Pour the sauce over the hot broccoli and stir gently to coat. Serve warm.

---— CHEF'S NOTE ———

This sauce tastes great served over steamed kale, too!

Jazzy Tip: To make broccoli, kale, or other green veggies more appealing, simply serve them in a sweet sauce. Here is a syrupy sauce to use as a tasty topper for any cooked veggies: Whisk together 2 tablespoons maple syrup with 2 teaspoons reduced-sodium tamari. Toss with any hot, cooked veggies. It's jazzylicious!

Green Beans Almondine

[MAKES 4 TO 6 SERVINGS] Steamed green beans mixed with crunchy almonds make an excellent accompaniment to any holiday dinner. This snappy side serves well alongside a simple weeknight entrée too.

---

5 to 6 cups green beans, washed and ends removed
1 to 2 cups sweet red pepper, thinly sliced
¾ cup sliced or slivered almonds
1 tablespoon extra-virgin olive oil
1 teaspoon Italian seasoning or all-purpose seasoning
1 clove garlic, minced
1 teaspoon vegan margarine

Fit a steamer basket into a large sauce pan with a tight-fitting lid. Add 2 inches of cold water, then add the green beans. Cover and bring to a boil. Steam for 5 minutes. Add the red pepper slices and continue to steam until crisp-tender.

Meanwhile, put the almonds and olive oil in a medium sauté pan. Top with Italian or all-purpose seasoning and sauté over medium-low heat until slightly golden. Add the garlic and cook for 2 minutes. Add the vegan margarine and heat through. Remove from heat.

Put the steamed beans and peppers in a medium bowl. Pour the almond mixture over the top of the beans and toss to combine. Serve warm.

Steamed Green Beans and Carrots with Orange Sauce

[MAKES 4 SERVINGS] [NO OIL] The refreshing citrus notes of the orange juice enhance this colorful green beans and carrots combo. A finishing sprinkle of *gomasio* adds a subtle crunch, but if you cannot find *gomasio* in your market, plain toasted (or raw) hulled sesame seeds substitute perfectly.

---

4 carrots, scrubbed and sliced into sticks
3 cups green beans, cleaned and trimmed
2 tablespoons orange juice (freshly squeezed or store-bought)
1 tablespoon freshly squeezed lemon juice
1 teaspoon maple syrup
2 teaspoons *gomasio* (optional)

> ## CHEF'S NOTE
>
> For a completely oil-free recipe, eliminate optional *gomasio*.

Fit a steamer basket into a large sauce pan with a tight-fitting lid. Add 2 inches of cold water, then add the carrots. Cover and bring to a boil. Steam for 5 minutes. Add the green beans, cover, and steam for 6 to 7 minutes more, or until the carrots and beans are crisp-tender.

Meanwhile, put the orange juice, lemon juice, and maple syrup in a small bowl. Whisk to combine.

Transfer the cooked carrots and beans to a medium bowl. Add the sauce and toss to coat. Sprinkle with the *gomasio* (if using), toss lightly, and serve.

Maple-Baked Acorn Squash

[MAKES 4 SERVINGS] [NUT FREE] Here I have jazzed up my mom's delicious recipe that was a childhood favorite. I have used maple syrup instead of brown sugar and provided the option of adding pumpkin pie spice instead of cinnamon.

2 small acorn squash, halved and seeded

3 tablespoons maple syrup

2 teaspoons vegan margarine

1 teaspoon ground cinnamon or Mom's Pumpkin Pie Spice (page 60)

Preheat the oven to 400 degrees F. Line a rimmed baking pan with unbleached parchment paper.

Put the acorn squash halves, cut-side-up, on the prepared baking pan. Put 2 heaping teaspoons maple syrup, ½ teaspoon margarine, and ¼ teaspoon cinnamon or pumpkin pie spice in the center of each squash.

Tent with foil and bake 45 to 50 minutes or until the squash is soft and filling is bubbling.

Basic Baked Potatoes

[MAKES 4 SERVINGS] [NUT FREE, NO OIL] I know—you're thinking, "She even has a special way to bake potatoes?" Well, yes, I do! I love, love, love baked spuds and I have tried many different baking methods over the years. I find that by using the method described here, I end up with the perfect baked potato every time: moist and fluffy on the inside with slightly crispy skin on the outside. I hope you'll give it a try!

---

4 large russet potatoes, scrubbed,
   dark spots removed

Preheat the oven to 400 degrees F. Carve an X on the top of each potato to allow steam to escape during baking. Place the potatoes directly on the center rack of the oven, cut side facing up. Bake for about 1 hour, until crispy on the outside and slightly soft when squeezed. Using pot holders, remove the potatoes from the oven and put them on a large plate or wire rack. Cool slightly and serve!

Mashed Millet and Cauliflower

[MAKES 6 SERVINGS] [NUT FREE, NO OIL] Millet and cauliflower are combined to make this snazzy side dish that resembles mashed potatoes. It's a fresh twist on a classic dish.

---

1 small cauliflower, cut into small
   florets
1 cup millet, rinsed and drained
2¼ cups vegetable broth
Sea salt, to taste
Freshly ground pepper, to taste

Put the cauliflower, millet, and broth in a medium sauce pan and bring to a boil over medium heat. Decrease the heat to medium-low, cover, and simmer for 25 minutes or until the liquid is absorbed and the cauliflower and millet are both very soft. Remove from the heat, cover, and let stand for 5 minutes. Transfer the cauliflower and millet to a medium bowl and mash using a potato masher until the consistency of mashed potatoes is achieved. Sprinkle with salt and pepper. Serve hot.

Paprika Roasted Cauliflower

[MAKES 4 TO 6 SERVINGS] [NUT FREE] A punch of paprika dresses up cauliflower, while roasting it brings out the sweet, rustic flavor of this sometimes-shunned veggie. The olive oil may be omitted from this dish, but it does add a pleasing pop of flavor and texture.

---

1 medium head of cauliflower, cut into bite-size florets
1 medium red or yellow onion, thinly sliced
1 tablespoon extra-virgin olive oil (optional)
2 teaspoons Italian seasoning
1 teaspoon garlic powder
1 teaspoon paprika
½ teaspoon turmeric

Preheat the oven to 400 degrees F. Line a large, rimmed baking pan with unbleached parchment paper.

Put all of the ingredients in a large bowl. Stir to combine. Spread the mixture in an even layer on the lined baking pan.

Bake for 45 to 55 minutes, until the cauliflower is tender but still holds its shape. Serve warm, room-temperature, or chilled.

— CHEF'S NOTE —

[NO OIL] For a completely oil-free recipe, omit the optional olive oil.

Paprika and Rosemary Roasted Red Potatoes

[MAKES 3 TO 4 SERVINGS] [NUT FREE] Rosemary is an herb that my grandma often used when flavoring potatoes. Here I have jazzed it up a bit by including paprika, which adds a pop of color and taste to this festive side dish.

6 medium red potatoes, scrubbed and cut in half
2 teaspoons extra-virgin olive oil
1 teaspoon crushed dried rosemary
½ teaspoon paprika
½ teaspoon garlic powder
¼ teaspoon sea salt
⅛ teaspoon freshly ground pepper

Preheat the oven to 400 degrees F. Line a large, rimmed baking pan with unbleached parchment paper.

Put the potatoes, olive oil, rosemary, paprika, garlic powder, salt, and pepper in a large mixing bowl and toss until coated. Transfer the potatoes to the prepared pan. Bake for 50 minutes to 1 hour, stirring once or twice, until potatoes are soft to the touch and slightly golden.

Twice-Baked Potatoes

[MAKES 6 SERVINGS] [NUT FREE, NO OIL] Both my grandma and my mom often made twice-baked potatoes and I just loved them! Because it was one of my favorite dishes as a child, I set out to create an equally delectable spud, stuffed with a smooth and savory filling that is reminiscent of childhood culinary bliss!

---

3 very large russet potatoes, scrubbed, baked, and cooled (see note and see page 209)
1 cup cooked white beans (drained and rinsed if canned)
¼ cup nondairy milk, plus more as needed
⅛ teaspoon garlic powder
⅛ teaspoon sea salt or Himalayan pink salt, plus more as needed
2 tablespoons minced onion
2 tablespoons diced sweet red pepper
½ teaspoon paprika
¼ teaspoon Italian seasoning
Freshly ground pepper, to taste

CHEF'S NOTE

The russet potatoes may be baked up to 24 hours in advance of preparing this recipe. After they have cooled, wrap them tightly in foil and store them in the refrigerator until use.

Preheat the oven to 375 degrees F. Line a small, rimmed baking pan with unbleached parchment paper.

Slice each potato in half lengthwise. Carefully scoop out the pulp, using a teaspoon or grapefruit spoon, leaving about ¼ inch of the potato skin and pulp intact. Put the potato pulp, white beans, nondairy milk, garlic powder, and ⅛ teaspoon salt in a high-performance blending appliance and process until smooth. If the mixture is still lumpy, add more nondairy milk, 1 tablespoon at a time, to achieve a smooth consistency. Put the potato mixture in a medium bowl. Gently stir in the onion and pepper. Using a large spoon or piping bag, spoon or pipe one-sixth of the potato mixture into each potato skin. Place the potato on the prepared baking pan. Repeat until all of the potato skins are filled. Sprinkle the tops of each potato with paprika, Italian seasoning, salt, and pepper to taste.

Tent the baking pan with foil and bake for 40 minutes. Uncover and bake for 15 to 20 minutes or until the tops are crispy and slightly golden. Cool for 5 to 7 minutes and serve.

Confetti Oven Fries

[MAKES 3 TO 4 SERVINGS] [NUT FREE] Craving French fries? This tempting mix of russets and sweet potatoes turns into delicious "fries" when tossed with a tiny bit of olive oil and baked in the oven. Fun food at its best!

---

2 large russet potatoes, scrubbed
2 large sweet potatoes, scrubbed
½ to 1 tablespoon extra-virgin olive oil
1 teaspoon Italian seasoning or all-purpose seasoning
¾ teaspoon chili powder
¾ teaspoon garlic powder
½ teaspoon sea salt, plus more as needed

Preheat the oven to 400 degrees F. Line a large, rimmed baking sheet with parchment paper.

Cut the potatoes into matchsticks or shoestrings; the thinner they are, the crispier the fries will be. Put the potatoes, olive oil, Italian or all-purpose seasoning, chili powder, and garlic powder in a large bowl and toss gently until the potatoes are evenly coated.

Spread the potatoes in a single layer on the lined baking sheet. Bake for 25 minutes and remove from the oven. Sprinkle with salt and stir gently to coat. Bake for an additional 15 to 20 minutes or until soft inside, slightly crisp outside, and browned along the edges. Season to taste with additional sea salt, if desired. Serve immediately.

Mashed Potatoes with Roasted Garlic

[MAKES 4 TO 5 SERVINGS] [NUT FREE] Mashed potatoes are a classic comfort food. I have given them a lively makeover with the addition of baked garlic, which adds delicious flavor to these mashed spuds.

3 cloves garlic, chopped
½ teaspoon extra-virgin olive oil
5 large white potatoes
2 tablespoons unsweetened nondairy
    milk, plus more as needed
1 tablespoon vegan mayonnaise or
    plain vegan yogurt (optional)
½ teaspoon Italian seasoning
¼ teaspoon sea salt
Freshly ground pepper, to taste
Chopped fresh flat-leaf parsley, for
    garnish (optional)

Preheat the oven to 400 degrees F. Put the garlic in the center of a 12-inch square of aluminum foil. Drizzle with the olive oil. Wrap the garlic in the foil, crimping the edges to make a tight seal. Bake for 15 to 20 minutes, until golden and soft.

While the garlic bakes, fit a steamer basket into a large sauce pan with a tight-fitting lid. Add 2 inches of cold water, then add the potatoes. Cover and bring to a boil. Steam the potatoes for 16 to 18 minutes, until they are soft but not mushy.

Meanwhile, heat the nondairy milk in a small sauce pan over medium-low heat until it's steaming hot but not boiling. Transfer the steamed potatoes to a medium bowl and add the baked garlic, nondairy milk, vegan mayonnaise or vegan yogurt (if using), Italian seasoning, and salt. Mash with a potato masher until smooth and lump-free, adding more nondairy milk as needed to achieve the desired consistency. Season with pepper. Serve immediately, garnished with parsley, if desired.

Quick Quinoa

[MAKES 4 SERVINGS] [NUT FREE] Quinoa has a delicious, nutty taste and makes a great substitute for brown rice in most any meal. It is quick to prepare, cooking in about 15 minutes!

1 cup white quinoa, rinsed and drained (see note)
2 cups filtered or spring water
1 vegetable bouillon cube, crumbled (see note)
2 tablespoons chopped fresh flat-leaf parsley (optional, plus more for garnish)

Put the quinoa, water, and crumbled bouillon cube in a medium sauce pan. Cover and bring to a boil over medium heat. Decrease the heat to medium-low and continue to simmer for 15 to 17 minutes or until the liquid is absorbed. Fluff with a fork. Stir in 2 tablespoons of parsley (if using). Cover, and let stand for 5 minutes. Sprinkle more parsley (if using) over the top and serve!

CHEF'S NOTES

Quinoa must be rinsed well before cooking. One way of doing this is to place your quinoa in a large bowl after it has been measured for the recipe. Cover the quinoa with cold water and swish it around with your hands or a large spoon. Pour it into a fine mesh colander, then run cold water over and through it for about 15 seconds. Rinse again with cold water until the water runs clear. Your quinoa is now ready to use in any recipe.

[NO OIL] For a completely oil-free recipe, use 2 cups nonfat vegetable broth instead of water and bouillon cube.

Black Quinoa with Cremini Mushrooms

[MAKES 4 TO 5 SERVINGS] [NUT FREE] In this dish, mushrooms add robust flavor to black quinoa, which is reminiscent of "forbidden rice." Black quinoa is becoming more popular these days, but if you cannot locate it in your supermarket, you may use the white or red variety in this novel side dish.

---

3 cups sliced cremini or white
    button mushrooms
½ teaspoon tamari
2½ cups filtered or spring water,
    plus more as needed
1 cup black quinoa, rinsed and
    drained (see note)
1 vegetable bouillon cube, crumbled

CHEF'S NOTE

You may use white or red quinoa in place of the black quinoa. When cooking white or red quinoa in this recipe, decrease the water by ¼ cup and decrease the cooking time by 4 to 6 minutes.

Put the mushrooms, tamari, and 2 tablespoons water in a medium sauce pan. Cook the mushrooms over medium heat for 2 to 3 minutes. Add more water, 2 tablespoons at a time as needed, to keep the mushrooms from sticking to the bottom of the pan. The mushroom mixture should be very wet at this point.

Add the quinoa, crumbled bouillon cube, and 2¼ cups water to the mushrooms. Cover tightly and decrease the heat to medium-low. Bring to a simmer and cook for 18 to 20 minutes until all of the liquid has been absorbed. If the quinoa is not completely soft at this point, add another ¼ cup water and continue to cook for an additional 3 to 5 minutes or until all of the liquid has been absorbed.

Remove from heat and fluff with a fork. Cover and let stand for 5 to 10 minutes before serving.

Chewy Chocolate Chip Cookies (page 226)

Chapter 12
Cookies, Cakes, and Confections

Do you know anyone who has a
real sweet tooth? Well, I sure do. In this
chapter I'll share my fabulous, jazzed-up
culinary confections. When the cookie
monster comes to call, you'll be ready with
cookielicious recipes that are oh-so-easy to
prepare. If baking cakes is on your mind,
you'll find satisfaction with my super yummy
vegan versions of several classic cake recipes.
I have also included my scrumptious, sugary
bites, featuring mouthwatering lollipops,
captivating chocolates, and tantalizing
truffles. It's time to prepare some sweets
for the sweet in your life!

"*If it sounds good and feels good, then it is good!*"

——Duke Ellington

Oatmeal Lace Cookies

[MAKES 10 TO 15 COOKIES] [NUT FREE] Quick to prepare and a delight to eat, these cookies make the perfect indulgence for your lunch box, an afternoon snack, or a flavorsome dessert.

1 cup rolled oats
1 cup "O's"-style cereal
1 teaspoon baking powder
½ teaspoon ground cinnamon
⅛ teaspoon sea salt
⅓ cup raisins
⅓ cup vegan chocolate chips
⅓ cup vegan margarine
3 tablespoons brown sugar
3 tablespoons organic unsulphured
    blackstrap molasses
½ teaspoon vanilla extract

Preheat the oven to 350 degrees F. Line a large baking sheet with unbleached parchment paper. Pour the oats into a blender and process until it resembles coarse flour. Transfer to a large bowl. Put the O's cereal in a blender and process into coarse crumbs. Transfer to a large bowl. Add the baking powder, cinnamon, and salt to the oat mixture and stir with a dry whisk to combine. Add the raisins and vegan chocolate chips and stir to coat.

Put the vegan margarine, sugar, molasses, and vanilla extract in a small bowl and stir until combined. Add the vegan margarine mixture to the dry ingredients and stir with a wooden spoon or mix with your hands until the ingredients are incorporated. Drop the batter by tablespoonfuls onto the prepared baking sheet, flattening with a flat spatula as you go.

Bake for 9 to 12 minutes, or until golden around the edges. Put the pan on a wire rack. Cookies will be *very* soft. Carefully transfer the entire sheet of parchment paper with the cookies still on it to a room-temperature baking sheet on a wire rack and allow the cookies to cool for 30 minutes. Stored in an airtight container in the refrigerator, the cookies will keep for 2 days.

Chewy Chocolate Chip Cookies

[MAKES 20 TO 24 LARGE COOKIES] Chewy and chocolaty, these tasty treats will surely satisfy your cookie cravings. If nuts are not part of your diet plan, simply leave them out. These baked delights will still be delicious!

2 cups whole-wheat flour
1 cup maple sugar
1 teaspoon baking soda
½ teaspoon baking powder
¼ teaspoon sea salt
1 cup pecans, roughly chopped
1 cup vegan chocolate chips (grain-sweetened variety works well)
1½ cups fresh apple purée (see note)
1 teaspoon vanilla extract
⅓ cup plus 2 tablespoons nondairy milk

CHEF'S NOTE

To make the apple purée, peel and core 3 very large or 4 medium apples. Rough chop the apples. Put the apples in a blender and process until the consistency of smooth applesauce is achieved. Be careful not to liquefy!

Preheat the oven to 375 degrees F. Line a large baking sheet with unbleached parchment paper.

Put the flour, maple sugar, baking soda, baking powder, and salt in a large bowl and stir with a dry whisk to combine. Add the pecans and vegan chocolate chips, and stir with the whisk to combine. Stir in the apple purée, vanilla extract, and nondairy milk, and mix just until incorporated. If the dough seems overly wet, stir in a bit more flour, 1 tablespoon at a time. Alternately, if the dough seems overly dry, stir in a bit more nondairy milk, 1 tablespoon at a time.

For each cookie, drop about 2½ tablespoons of the dough onto the prepared baking sheet. Flatten slightly using the back of a flat spatula.

Bake 15 to 18 minutes, or until slightly golden around the edges. Remove the sheet from the oven and let cool for 2 minutes. Transfer cookies to a wire rack. Cool for about 10 minutes. Stored in an airtight container in the refrigerator, the cookies will keep for about 2 days.

Peanut Butter and Jelly Cookies

[MAKES 18 COOKIES] Like peanut butter and jelly sandwiches packed into sweet cookie confections, these gems truly shine. With a delectable jelly center and crisp base, they make the perfect afternoon snack paired with a tall glass of nondairy milk.

---

1 cup whole-wheat flour
½ teaspoon baking powder
⅛ teaspoon sea salt
⅓ cup creamy peanut butter
⅓ cup maple syrup
3 tablespoons nondairy milk
1 teaspoon vanilla extract
½ to ⅔ cup raspberry, strawberry,
    or blueberry preserves, jelly,
    or jam

Preheat the oven to 375 degrees F. Line a large baking sheet with unbleached parchment paper.

Put the flour, baking powder, and salt in a medium bowl and stir with a dry whisk to combine. Add the peanut butter, maple syrup, nondairy milk, and vanilla extract to the flour mixture and stir vigorously until smooth and well combined. The dough will be stiff.

For each cookie, drop about 1 tablespoon of the dough onto the prepared baking sheet, using a cookie scoop or rounded spoon. With your thumb, press down gently into the middle of each cookie, making a small well. Fill each well with 1 teaspoon of the preserves.

Bake for 16 to 18 minutes, or until the cookies are golden brown around the edges. Put the baking sheet on a wire rack. Let the cookies cool on the baking sheet for 15 minutes before transferring to a serving platter to further cool. Stored in an airtight container in the refrigerator, the cookies will keep for about 3 days.

Mom's Turtle Cookie Squares

[MAKES 16 TO 20 COOKIES] For years, my mom has been making a dairy-based version of these cookies for the holidays. Several years ago we decided to create a vegan version, which is as good as—or maybe even better than—the original recipe.

CRUST
½ cup vegan margarine
1 cup brown sugar, firmly packed
1 cup whole-wheat flour
1 cup pecan halves

FILLING
⅔ cup vegan margarine
½ cup brown sugar, firmly packed

FROSTING
1½ cups vegan chocolate chips

Preheat the oven to 350 degrees F. To make the crust, put ½ cup vegan margarine, 1 cup brown sugar, and flour in a high-performance blending appliance and process until particles are fine, forming a loose dough. Pour into a nonstick, ungreased 8 x 12 inch baking pan. Press the dough into an even layer, using your hands. Arrange the pecan halves evenly over the unbaked crust.

To make the filling, put ⅔ cup vegan margarine and ½ cup brown sugar in a small sauce pan. Cook over medium-low heat, stirring constantly, until the sugar dissolves and the mixture starts to bubble. Pour the hot filling over the pecans and crust. Bake on the center rack of the oven for 18 to 20 minutes until the pecans are slightly golden.

Put the pan on a wire rack and immediately pour the vegan chocolate chips over the pecans and filling. As the chips melt, spread the chocolate evenly over the top of the pecans and filling. (If the chocolate chips do not melt completely, put the pan back in the oven for 30 seconds to 1 minute to melt.)

Cool for 30 minutes and cut into 16 to 20 cookie squares. Stored in an airtight container in the refrigerator, the cookies will keep for 4 days.

Coconut Vegaroons

[MAKES 24 COOKIES] Flaxseeds stand in for the egg whites in this recipe, while garbanzo bean flour helps to bind them. The result is a flawless macaroon that is egg-, dairy-, *and* gluten-free! Now *that* is jazzy.

---

2 tablespoons golden flaxseeds
¼ cup plus 1 tablespoon filtered or spring water
1⅓ cups raw unsweetened shredded dried coconut
½ cup plus 2 tablespoons maple sugar
2 tablespoons garbanzo bean (chickpea) flour
⅛ teaspoon sea salt
2 tablespoons nondairy milk
1¼ teaspoons vanilla extract

Preheat the oven to 325 degrees F. Line a large baking sheet with unbleached parchment paper.

Put the flaxseeds in a high-performance blender or grain mill and process into a very fine flour. Transfer to a small bowl. Stir in the water and whisk vigorously to combine. Let the flaxseed mixture stand for 10 minutes while prepping the rest of the ingredients.

Put the coconut, maple sugar, garbanzo bean flour, and salt in a large bowl and stir with a dry whisk to combine. Add the flaxseed mixture, nondairy milk, and vanilla extract, and stir until well blended. For each cookie, drop 1 heaping tablespoonful of the dough onto the lined baking sheet with a cookie scoop or rounded spoon, spacing them about 1 inch apart. Flatten each macaroon slightly using a flat spatula. Bake for 15 minutes. Decrease the temperature to 300 degrees F and bake for 12 to 15 minutes, or until slightly golden brown.

Put the baking sheet on a wire rack. Let the cookies cool on the baking sheet for 5 minutes before transferring to a serving platter to cool completely. Stored in an airtight container in the refrigerator, the cookies will keep for 4 days.

Holiday Sandies Cookies

[MAKES 24 TO 26 COOKIES] My grandma made a butter-based version of these cookies every holiday, and now my mom has followed suit. As a child, I used to sneak these cookies right off of the dessert tray, even before dinner was served! This jazzy, nondairy version is every bit as good as Grandma's . . . and no one will *ever* suspect that it's vegan!

COOKIES
1 cup homemade oat flour (see note)
½ cup ground walnuts (see note)
2 tablespoons vegan confectioners' sugar
6 tablespoons cold vegan margarine
1 teaspoon vanilla extract
2 to 2½ teaspoons cold nondairy milk

TOPPING
½ cup vegan confectioners' sugar

---- CHEF'S NOTES ----

To make oat flour, place 1½ cups rolled oats in a blender and process into a coarse flour. Proceed with recipe as directed.

To grind walnuts, place ¾ cup chopped walnuts in a blender and process into coarse crumbs. Proceed with recipe as directed.

Preheat the oven to 350 degrees F. Line a large baking sheet with unbleached parchment paper.

Put the oat flour, walnuts, and 2 tablespoons confectioners' sugar in a medium bowl and stir with a dry whisk to combine. Add the vegan margarine and vanilla. Mix to combine using a dough blender or large fork. Add the nondairy milk, 1 teaspoon at a time, until the mixture becomes the consistency of soft dough.

Form the dough into a log. Cover the log loosely in parchment paper, and refrigerate for 20 to 30 minutes, or until almost firm to the touch. Cut a ¼-inch slice from the dough log. Put the slice on the lined baking sheet and form it into a crescent shape. Repeat with the remaining dough, until you have formed 24 to 26 cookies. Bake for 7 minutes, then turn the heat down to 300 degrees F. Bake 10 to 12 minutes more, or until the cookies are slightly golden around the edges. Put the baking sheet on a wire rack and cool for 3 to 4 minutes.

Pour ½ cup confectioners' sugar into a small bowl. Roll each cookie in the confectioners' sugar. Arrange the cookies on a pretty serving tray. Stored in an airtight container in the refrigerator, the cookies will keep for 4 days.

No-Bake Peanut Butter Cookies

[MAKES 16 COOKIES] These cookies make a great warm-weather treat since they do not require baking! This easy-to-prepare treat is a great recipe to make with children's help.

1 cup vegan cookie crumbs or vegan
  graham cracker crumbs
½ cup chopped walnuts
⅓ cup raisins
4 to 5 tablespoons peanut butter
  (creamy or chunky)
3 tablespoons brown rice syrup

Line a large baking sheet with unbleached parchment paper. Put all of the ingredients in a medium bowl. Mix together with your hands until all of the ingredients are incorporated. The dough will be very stiff. For each cookie, drop 1 tablespoon of the dough onto the lined baking sheet using a cookie scoop or spoon. Firmly press the cookies into a dome shape, using your hands to help them hold together. Refrigerate for 2 to 4 hours, or until the cookies have set.

Coconut-Date Truffles

[MAKES 14 TRUFFLES] I made these beauties for Michael Feinstein when filming his interview for the television show and he loved them! I know you'll love them too.

6 large Medjool dates
3 heaping tablespoons raisins
2 tablespoons unsweetened
  shredded dried coconut
2 tablespoons raw sunflower seeds
2 tablespoons unsweetened cocoa
  powder

Line a small baking sheet with unbleached parchment paper. Put the dates, raisins, coconut, and sunflower seeds in a high-performance blender and process to the consistency of soft dough. Transfer the date mixture to a medium bowl. Spoon out a heaping tablespoon of the date mixture, and roll it into a ball. Put the cocoa powder in a small bowl. Roll each truffle in the cocoa powder until coated and place on the prepared sheet. Refrigerate for 1 hour. Store truffles in an airtight container in the refrigerator.

Chocolate Candy Clusters

[MAKES 12 TO 14 CANDIES] These quick-to-craft candies are so easy to make, yet they are bursting with rich flavor. Use your favorite ready-to-eat granola or cluster-style breakfast cereal in this recipe.

5 heaping tablespoons vegan dark chocolate chips
1 cup ready-to-eat vegan cluster-style cereal or granola
1 tablespoon raw unsweetened shredded dried coconut

CHEF'S NOTE

If you don't have a double boiler, you can improvise one with a heatproof bowl and a sauce pan. The bowl should partially (not completely) fit into the sauce pan. Fill the sauce pan with enough water so that when the bowl rests in the sauce pan, the water doesn't touch the bottom of the bowl. Bring the water to a simmer. Put the ingredients in the bowl, and place the bowl in the sauce pan.

Line a medium baking sheet with unbleached parchment paper. Put the vegan chocolate chips in a double boiler over medium-low heat (see note). When the chocolate has melted, remove from the heat.

Put the cereal in a medium bowl. Pour the melted chocolate over the cereal and stir together until the chocolate completely coats the cereal.

For each cluster, drop 1 heaping tablespoon of the chocolate mixture on the lined baking sheet. Sprinkle a bit of coconut over the top of each cluster. Cover and refrigerate for 30 minutes, or until set. Stored in an airtight container in the refrigerator, clusters will keep for about 5 days.

Chocolate Ganache Cake

[MAKES 8 SERVINGS] [NUT FREE] This is a rich, decadent-tasting, and gorgeous cake. This scrumptious confection, topped with a luscious vegan chocolate ganache frosting, is ideal to serve as an enticing dessert at any gathering throughout the year.

CAKE
2 cups whole-wheat pastry flour
⅔ cup unsweetened cocoa powder
1 teaspoon baking powder
1 teaspoon baking soda
½ teaspoon sea salt
1¼ cups brown sugar
1½ cups chocolate- or vanilla-
    flavored nondairy milk, plus
    more as needed
¼ cup vegan cream cheese, at room
    temperature
¼ cup extra-virgin olive oil
1 teaspoon vanilla extract

GANACHE
½ cup nondairy milk (a thicker
    variety works best)
1 bar (3.5 ounces) vegan dark
    chocolate (snack-style bar, *not*
    unsweetened baking chocolate)
1 teaspoon extra-virgin olive oil
1 tablespoon brown sugar

Preheat the oven to 400 degrees F.

Lightly coat a 9-inch round baking pan with vegan margarine. Put the flour, cocoa powder, baking powder, baking soda, and salt in a large bowl and stir with a dry whisk to combine. Add the brown sugar and whisk to combine. Put ¼ cup of the nondairy milk, vegan cream cheese, olive oil, and vanilla extract in a blender and process until smooth. Add to the flour mixture, along with the remaining 1¼ cups of nondairy milk. Stir until well combined and somewhat fluffy. The mixture will be stiff, but if it seems overly dry, stir in additional nondairy milk, 1 tablespoon at a time, up to 3 tablespoons. Pour the mixture into the prepared pan and smooth the top. Bake for 15 minutes. Decrease the heat to 350 degrees F and bake for 25 minutes, or until a toothpick inserted in the center comes out clean. (If it seems that the cake is starting to burn during the last 10 minutes of baking, tent it with foil.) Put the pan on a wire rack. Allow the cake to cool completely.

While the cake is cooling, prepare the ganache. Heat the nondairy milk in a small sauce pan over medium-low heat until steaming hot but not boiling. Chop the vegan chocolate bar into small pieces. Put the chocolate pieces, olive oil and sugar in a large bowl. Slowly pour in the nondairy milk, 2 to 3 tablespoons at a time, whisking

vigorously after each addition, until the chocolate is smooth and shiny. Immediately drizzle or spread the frosting over the cake. Refrigerate for 1 hour or until set. Covered tightly and stored in the refrigerator, leftover cake will keep for about 2 days.

German Chocolate Cake

[MAKES 10 SERVINGS] My grandma made a German chocolate cake that was simply out of this world. I adored it and so I have created a vegan version that tastes much like the original.

FROSTING

⅓ cup vegan margarine
½ cup (about 4 ounces) soft regular tofu, drained
¼ cup maple syrup
1 teaspoon vanilla extract
1 cup raw unsweetened shredded dried coconut
¾ cup chopped pecans
3 tablespoons maple sugar

CAKE

1 cup whole-wheat flour
1 cup pastry flour
1 teaspoon baking powder
1 teaspoon baking soda
¼ teaspoon sea salt
¾ cup maple sugar
½ cup unsweetened cocoa powder
¼ cup unsweetened shredded dried coconut
1¼ cups sweetened nondairy milk
2 tablespoons extra-virgin olive oil
1 tablespoon freshly squeezed lemon juice
10 whole pecans for garnish (optional)
¼ cup vegan chocolate curls (see note, page 256)

To make the frosting, put the vegan margarine, tofu, maple syrup, and vanilla extract in a blender and process until smooth. Transfer to a medium bowl. Add the coconut, pecans, and maple sugar and stir until well blended. Cover and refrigerate for 2 to 3 hours.

Preheat the oven to 375 degrees F. Oil a 9-inch round cake pan. Put the flours, baking powder, baking soda, and salt in a large bowl and stir with a dry whisk to combine. Add the maple sugar, cocoa powder, and coconut, and whisk to combine. Stir in the nondairy milk, olive oil, and lemon juice and mix just until incorporated. Don't overmix or the cake will be tough. Pour into the prepared cake pan. Bake for 30 to 35 minutes, until a toothpick inserted in the middle of the cake comes out clean. Put the pan on a wire rack and loosen the sides of the cake with a knife. Cool for about 15 minutes. Carefully remove the cake from the pan. Let the cake cool completely for about 1 hour before frosting.

Spoon the frosting over the top of the cake. Gently spread the frosting in an even layer, using an offset spatula (the frosting will be *very* thick). Garnish with pecans and vegan chocolate curls (if using). Serve at room temperature or chilled. Covered tightly and stored in the refrigerator, the cake will keep for 2 days.

Lovely Lemon Cake

[MAKES 8 SERVINGS] [NUT FREE] Light, lemony, and truly lovely, this appealing cake is ready for the oven in about 10 minutes! Bake it for 40 minutes and you'll have a homemade cake for after supper!

2 cups whole-wheat flour

2 teaspoons baking powder

1 teaspoon baking soda

½ teaspoon sea salt

1 cup brown sugar or maple sugar

½ cup vegan margarine, melted

2 teaspoons packed lemon zest (zest of about ½ large lemon)

2 tablespoons freshly squeezed lemon juice

1½ cups sweetened nondairy milk

¼ cup vegan confectioners' sugar, plus more as needed

3 or 4 large strawberries, sliced lengthwise into "fans," for garnish (optional)

Additional lemon zest, for garnish (optional)

Preheat the oven to 375 degrees F. Oil a 9-inch round cake pan. Put the flour, baking powder, baking soda, and salt in a large bowl and stir with a dry whisk to combine. Add the sugar and whisk to combine. Add the vegan margarine, lemon zest, lemon juice, and nondairy milk and stir just until incorporated. Pour the batter into the prepared pan and smooth the top.

Bake for 40 minutes, or until a toothpick inserted in the center of the cake comes out clean. (If the cake is browning too much, tent the top with foil during the last 10 to 15 minutes of baking.)

Put the pan on a wire rack and loosen the sides with a knife. Cool for 15 minutes. Invert onto a pretty serving plate and dust liberally with confectioners' sugar. Garnish with strawberry fans and lemon zest, if desired.

Blueberry Cheeze-Cake

[MAKES 6 TO 8 SERVINGS] [NUT FREE] This delectable and creamy-tasting treat has a "melt-in-your-mouth" texture that resembles a rich cream- and egg-laden dessert. The delicate, semisweet flavor makes a welcome finish to any merry meal; however, the cake is so easy to prepare that you may find yourself serving this cheeze-y confection as a weeknight treat on a regular basis!

CRUST
¾ cup packed vegan cookie crumbs
    (ginger cookies are nice for this,
    see note)
2½ tablespoons vegan margarine

FILLING
20 ounces firm regular tofu,
    drained
¾ cup maple sugar
2 teaspoons vanilla extract

TOPPING
1 cup fresh or frozen blueberries
¼ cup blueberry preserves
1 tablespoon maple sugar

CHEF'S NOTE

To make cookie crumbs, put about 1½ cups of broken cookies in a blender, and process to coarse crumbs.

Preheat the oven to 375 degrees F.

To make the crust, put the cookie crumbs and the vegan margarine in a medium bowl and stir until incorporated. Press the crumb mixture evenly into the bottom of a 9-inch round springform pan. For the filling, put the tofu, sugar, and vanilla extract in a blender and process until smooth. Pour the tofu mixture over the crust. Spread in an even layer and smooth the top. Bake for 30 to 40 minutes, or until the center of the cake is firm to the touch. Put the pan on a wire rack. Carefully run a table knife around the perimeter of the cake to ensure it does not stick to the side of the pan. Let the cake cool for 10 minutes, or until slightly firm. Release the side of the springform pan to unmold.

Meanwhile, put the blueberries, preserves, and sugar in a small sauce pan. Bring to a simmer over medium-low heat and cook for 10 to 15 minutes, until slightly reduced and thickened. Spoon the blueberry topping over the cake, spreading it evenly over the top. Refrigerate the cake for at least 2 hours before serving. Covered loosely with plastic wrap and stored in the refrigerator, the cake will keep for about 2 days.

Zucchini-Orange Cupcakes with Vanilla Cream Cheese Frosting

[MAKES 6 GIANT CUPCAKES] [NUT FREE] It's cupcake time! In this mouthwatering baked treat, orange juice stands in for nondairy milk, and shredded zucchini adds moisture and volume. If you serve the cupcakes sans the vegan frosting, these tasty delights make a great low-fat breakfast muffin or afternoon snack. Add the frosting and they make a "once-in-a-while" confection that will surely please any hard-core cupcake fan!

FROSTING
8 ounces vegan cream cheese

4 tablespoons vegan margarine

½ cup vegan confectioners' sugar, plus more as needed

1½ teaspoons vanilla extract

CUPCAKES
2 cups whole-wheat flour

2 teaspoons baking soda

½ teaspoon baking powder

⅓ cup brown sugar

1 cup grated zucchini, drained (see note, page 100)

½ cup dried cherries

1¼ cups freshly squeezed or refrigerated store-bought orange juice

1 tablespoon orange zest, for garnish

Preheat the oven to 375 degrees F. Line a 6-cup standard muffin tin with paper liners.

To make the frosting, put the vegan cream cheese, vegan margarine, confectioners' sugar, and vanilla extract in a medium bowl and stir vigorously until smooth and well blended. Taste and add more sugar, up to 1 tablespoon, if desired. Cover and refrigerate for 1 to 3 hours.

To make the cupcakes, put the flour, baking soda, and baking powder in a large bowl and stir with a whisk to combine. Add the brown sugar and whisk to combine. Stir in the zucchini and cherries. Add the orange juice and mix just until incorporated. Don't overmix or the cupcakes will be tough. Mound the mixture into the prepared tin. Put the pan on a baking sheet and bake for 30 to 35 minutes, or until golden and a toothpick inserted in the middle of a cupcake comes out clean. Put the pan on a wire rack. Cool for 10 minutes. Carefully remove the cupcakes from the muffin tin, and place them on the wire rack. Let the cupcakes cool completely.

Spoon or pipe a generous amount of frosting on top of each cupcake. Top with some orange zest, placed artfully in the center of the frosting. Covered tightly and stored in the refrigerator, leftover cupcakes will keep for about 2 days. Serve chilled or at room temperature.

Choco-Peanut Butter Cups

[MAKES 10 SERVINGS] I wanted to create an easy-to-make, vegan chocolate candy cup to take the place of the store-bought version that I used to love as a child. With a nice punch of peanut butter combined with luscious dark chocolate, these candies are sure to satisfy your chocolate cravings.

¾ cup vegan chocolate chips
⅓ cup creamy peanut butter
1 teaspoon maple syrup

Line a mini-muffin tin with 10 paper liners. Put the vegan chocolate chips in a double boiler over medium-low heat (see note, page 237). When the chocolate has melted, remove from the heat.

Put the peanut butter and maple syrup in a medium bowl and stir vigorously to thoroughly combine. Pour the chocolate into the peanut butter mixture and stir until smooth and well blended. Divide the chocolate–peanut butter mixture evenly among the prepared muffin cups. Smooth the tops using a rubber spatula or offset spatula.

Freeze for 20 minutes, then transfer to the refrigerator and refrigerate for at least 30 minutes more before serving. Serve chilled. Stored in an airtight container in the refrigerator, the clusters will keep for about 4 days.

Jazzy Tip: When creating compassionate chocolate confections, always use fair-trade, dairy-free dark chocolate. Using fair-trade chocolate supports equitable and sustainable trading partnerships, which create just opportunities that can help to alleviate poverty.

Chocolate Date-Nut Lollipops

[MAKES 8 TO 10 LOLLIPOPS] Fun, fun, fun! That's how I describe these lovely little lollipops! The dates help to hold the pops together while also standing in for much of the processed sugar. They're perfect for any party, whether you are entertaining kids or adults!

LOLLIPOPS
½ cup vegan dark chocolate chips (grain-sweetened variety works well)
6 large Medjool dates, pitted
¼ cup whole pecans
⅛ teaspoon vanilla extract

TOPPING
2 tablespoons ground pecans, walnuts, or hazelnuts (optional)
2 tablespoons dark, nondairy cocoa powder (optional)

Put the vegan chocolate chips in a double boiler over medium-low heat (see note, page 237). When the chocolate has melted, remove from the heat. Meanwhile, put the dates, pecans, and vanilla extract in a high-performance blending appliance and process to the consistency of soft dough. Transfer the date mixture to a medium bowl, pour in the melted chocolate, and stir until well combined. Put the date mixture in the freezer for 7 to 15 minutes or until the chocolate has set enough to roll into small balls.

Line a small baking sheet with unbleached parchment paper. Spoon out a heaping tablespoon of the chocolate mixture and quickly roll it into a ball. Roll it in one of the optional toppings until completely coated. Place it on the prepared baking sheet. Continue in this way, forming all of the remaining chocolate mixture into balls and coating them in one of the optional coatings.

Insert the end of a lollipop stick into each chocolate ball and place all lollipops upright in 2 separate mugs or shallow glasses, making sure they do not touch each other. Refrigerate for 1 to 2 hours before serving. For a festive presentation, wrap each lollipop in cellophane and tie with a pretty ribbon. Stored in an airtight container in the refrigerator, leftover lollipops will keep for up to 3 days.

Black Forest Pecan Pie
(page 258)

Chapter 13

Puddings, Pies, and Frozen Desserts

Preparing dairy- and egg-free puddings, pies, and frozen indulgences can be challenging. In this chapter I'll share how to make delicious, delectable, and luscious versions of these classic desserts. I have included flourless pie crusts, cream-less puddings, and frosty, frozen delights to savor any day of the week!

"If you have to ask what jazz is, you'll never know."

—Louis Armstrong

Almond "Creamy" Pudding

[MAKES 4 TO 6 SERVINGS] Got 5 minutes? That is all the time you need to prepare this rich and creamy-tasting pudding. The almond butter makes it super smooth and super yummy!

---

14 to 16 ounces soft or firm regular tofu, drained

6 heaping tablespoons almond butter

6 heaping tablespoons maple syrup

4 to 6 almonds, for garnish (optional)

Put the tofu, almond butter, and maple syrup in a blender and process until smooth and creamy. Spoon into 6 espresso cups, 4 martini glasses, or 4 small dessert dishes and refrigerate for 3 to 24 hours. Serve chilled, garnished with a whole almond on top, if desired.

Banana Milk-less Shake

[MAKES 2 TO 3 SERVINGS] [NUT FREE, NO OIL] This smooth shake will curb cravings if you desire a thick, frosty treat!

---

3 very large (or 4 small) frozen bananas (see note)

1½ cups chilled vanilla-flavored nondairy milk, plus more as needed

2 tablespoons maple syrup, plus more as needed

1 teaspoon vanilla extract

Put all of the ingredients in a blender and process until smooth and creamy. Taste and add more nondairy milk or maple syrup, if desired. Pour the mixture into pretty glasses.

--- CHEF'S NOTE ---

To freeze a banana, peel and cut it into 3 or 4 pieces and put them in a resealable freezer bag. Seal and freeze for at least 12 hours before using.

Chocolate Mousse Ginger Pie

[MAKES 8 SERVINGS] [NUT FREE] This pie is easy to prepare, gorgeous to look at, delicious to eat, and a delight to serve! It's the perfect pie for any festive occasion.

CRUST
2½ to 3 cups broken vegan ginger cookies (enough to make 1¾ cups crumbs)
½ cup vegan margarine, melted

FILLING
¾ cup vanilla-flavored nondairy milk
14 to 16 ounces soft regular or silken tofu, drained and broken up
2 bars (3.5 ounces each) vegan dark chocolate (snack bars, *not* unsweetened baking chocolate), finely chopped

GARNISH (optional)
½ vegan dark chocolate bar, cut into curls (see note)
10 to 15 raspberries (frozen raspberries work well for this)

Preheat the oven to 350 degrees F. Put the cookies in a blender and process into coarse crumbs. Put 1¾ cups of the crumbs in a medium bowl. Add the melted vegan margarine and stir to combine. Press the crust into an ungreased 9-inch pie plate. Bake for 10 minutes. Put the plate on a wire rack to cool.

Meanwhile, heat the nondairy milk in a small sauce pan over medium-low heat until steaming hot but not boiling. Put the tofu in a blender and then add the vegan chocolate pieces. Pour in the hot nondairy milk and process until completely smooth, about 1 minute. Pour the mousse into the prepared pie crust and smooth the top with a soft spatula.

Refrigerate for 4 hours or until set. To serve, garnish with chocolate curls and raspberries, if desired.

--- CHEF'S NOTE ---

To make chocolate curls, slice a vegan chocolate candy bar into small "curls" using a carrot peeler.

Black Forest Pecan Pie

[MAKES 8 SERVINGS] To finish any festive meal with a flourish, I take a cue from my mother, who always offered a homemade pecan pie as the finale for our holiday get-togethers. Now I have carried on that tradition with an innovative and tasty vegan version of this gooey, sweet treat that features a flourless crust. I must admit, I think this is the most decadent dessert I have ever created!

CRUST
10 large pitted Medjool dates
¾ cup rolled oats
¼ cup raw unsweetened shredded dried coconut
¼ cup pecan halves

FILLING
½ cup maple syrup
¼ cup unsulphured blackstrap molasses
1 cup vegan chocolate chips
5 pitted Medjool dates
2 tablespoons vegan margarine
2 tablespoons filtered or spring water
1 teaspoon vanilla extract
1½ cups whole pecans

TOPPING
15 whole pecans
Vanilla "Crème Fresh" (page 60) (optional)

Preheat the oven to 375 degrees F.

Put the dates, oats, coconut, and pecans in a high-performance blending appliance and process to the consistency of soft dough. Transfer the dough onto a board and form it into a ball. Flatten the dough slightly with your hands, and then use a rolling pin to roll the dough into a 10-inch round. Transfer the dough onto an ungreased 9-inch pie plate. Press the dough mixture evenly over the bottom of the plate, pushing it up the sides as you go, to make a crust. To craft a pretty edge to the crust, use your index finger to push the inner edge of the crust out, while pinching the outer edge in with the thumb and index finger of your other hand to make a classic scalloped edge around the pie crust.

Put the maple syrup, molasses, vegan chocolate chips, pitted dates, vegan margarine, water, and vanilla extract in a blender and process until very smooth. Pour the maple mixture in a medium bowl. Fold in 1½ cups whole pecans. Pour the filling into the crust and smooth the top using a rubber spatula. Gently press 15 whole pecans into the top of the pie, arranging

them in a pleasing manner. Put the pie on a baking sheet and bake for 25 to 30 minutes, or until the edges start to set and brown. Tent the pie with foil and bake for 5 to 8 minutes more, or until the pie has almost set in the middle. The filling will still be somewhat soft.

Carefully put the pie on a wire rack (the filling will be very hot!) and let cool for 1 hour. Cover and refrigerate for at least 2 hours. Serve chilled, topped with Vanilla "Crème Fresh" (if using). Cover and store leftover pie in the refrigerator for up to 3 days.

Pumpkin Pie with Date-Nut Crust

[MAKES 8 SERVINGS] This recipe follows in the footsteps of traditional pumpkin pie with a few jazzy twists. A delectable date, nut, and oat crust takes the place of the classic butter-and-flour version and the addition of vegan whipped cream makes it super festive. 'Tis the season for pumpkin pie!

CRUST
10 large pitted Medjool dates, plus more as needed
½ cup whole pecans
¾ cup rolled oats

FILLING
14 to 16 ounces firm regular tofu
1 can (about 16 ounces) pumpkin purée
⅔ cup maple sugar
1 tablespoon maple syrup
½ teaspoon vanilla extract
1½ teaspoons Mom's Pumpkin Pie Spice (page 60)
⅛ teaspoon sea salt

TOPPING
Bourbon Vanilla Whipped "Cream" (page 58) (optional)

CHEF'S NOTE
If desired, you may use a rolling pin to roll the dough into a 10-inch round before placing it in the pie plate.

Preheat the oven to 350 degrees F. Oil a 9-inch pie plate.

To make the crust, put the dates, pecans, and oats in a high-performance blending appliance and process until the mixture forms a dough. If the mixture is still too crumbly to hold together, add more pitted dates, one at a time, until the consistency is doughy. Form the date mixture into a ball and place it in the center of the prepared pie plate (see note). Press the date mixture evenly over the bottom of the plate, pushing it up the sides of the pie plate as you go, to make a crust. To craft a pretty edge to the crust, use your index finger to push the inner edge of the crust out, while pinching the outer edge in with the thumb and index finger of your other hand to make a classic scalloped edge around the pie crust.

Put all of the filling ingredients in a blender and process until smooth. Pour the filling into the crust and bake for 20 minutes. Remove the pie from the oven and cover the crust edges with small strips of foil. Bake the pie for 20 to 30 minutes more, or until the filling is somewhat firm to the touch (the center will still be slightly soft).

Place the pie on a wire rack to cool completely. Before serving, pipe whipped "cream" (if using)

around the perimeter of the pie using a star tip, or simply serve a dollop of the whipped "cream" on the side. If you are serving the pie warm, cool it at room temperature for 45 minutes to 1 hour before serving. If you are serving the pie chilled, cool, then cover it with foil and place it in the refrigerator for 3 to 24 hours before serving. Covered tightly and stored in the refrigerator, leftover pie will keep about 2 days.

Dreamy Banana Pie

[MAKE 8 SERVINGS] This pie is creamy, dreamy, and full of big banana flavor. The pie prepares in a flash and is great to serve at the close of any special meal or family get-together.

CRUST
⅔ cup raisins
1 cup rolled oats
½ cup pumpkin seeds
4 pitted Medjool dates
½ teaspoon ground cinnamon

FILLING
2 bananas
14 to 16 ounces soft silken tofu, drained
3 tablespoons maple syrup
3 tablespoons sesame tahini
1 teaspoon vanilla extract

TOPPING
1 tablespoon cocoa powder, plus more as needed
½ vegan dark chocolate bar, cut into curls, for garnish (optional) (see note, page 256)

Preheat the oven to 350 degrees F. Lightly oil a 9-inch round pie plate.

Put the raisins, oats, pumpkin seeds, dates, and cinnamon in a high-performance blending appliance and process on medium until a dough forms. Transfer the dough onto a board and form it into a ball. Flatten the dough slightly with your hands, and then use a rolling pin to roll the dough into a 10-inch round. Transfer the dough to an ungreased 9-inch pie plate. Press the dough mixture evenly over the bottom of the plate, pushing it up the sides of the pie plate as you go, to make a crust. Slice each banana into 10 to 12 slices and arrange the slices by overlapping them slightly on top of the crust.

Put the tofu, maple syrup, tahini, and vanilla extract in a blender and process until smooth. Pour the filling over the banana slices and smooth the top with a rubber spatula. Dust the top of the pie with the cocoa powder. Bake the pie for 30 to 40 minutes, or until the edges are firm. The center of the pie will still be slightly soft to the touch. Put the plate on a wire rack and cool for 30 minutes.

Just before serving, mound the chocolate curls (if using) in the center of the pie. Serve warm or chilled. Covered tightly and stored in the refrigerator, leftover pie will keep up to 24 hours.

Pear, Apple, and Walnut Crostata

[MAKES 6 TO 8 SERVINGS] Ground oats combined with walnuts, raisins, and shredded coconut make a quick, easy, and crisp crust for this delectable fruit pie. For the filling, juicy pears and apples get all dressed up with a dab of sugar—just enough to satisfy a sweet tooth!

CRUST
⅔ cup raisins
½ cup rolled oats
⅓ cup chopped walnuts
¼ cup unsweetened shredded
    dried coconut

FILLING
2 firm pears, peeled, cored, and sliced
1 large apple, peeled, cored, and
    sliced
⅓ cup chopped walnuts
2 heaping tablespoons brown sugar
    or maple sugar
2 heaping tablespoons maple syrup
½ teaspoon ground cinnamon

Preheat the oven to 375 degrees F. Oil a 9-inch pie plate.

To make the crust, put the raisins, oats, ⅓ cup walnuts, and coconut in a high-performance blending appliance and process until the mixture forms a dough. Transfer the dough to the prepared pie plate, and form it into a ball. Press the oat mixture evenly into the bottom and part of the way up the sides of the pie plate.

For the filling, put the pear slices, apple slices, ⅓ cup walnuts, maple sugar, 1 heaping tablespoon of brown sugar or maple syrup, and cinnamon in a large bowl and stir gently until combined. Pour the filling into the crust and spread it in an even layer, smoothing the top as you go. Bake the pie for 25 minutes.

Remove the pie and brush the top with the remaining 1 heaping tablespoon maple syrup. Tent the pie with foil and bake 10 to 20 minutes, until the fruit is softened and edges of crust are slightly golden. Cool 20 minutes and serve warm. Alternatively, refrigerate for 4 to 6 hours and serve the pie chilled. Covered tightly and stored in the refrigerator, leftover pie will keep about 2 days.

Apple Turnovers

[MAKES 4 SERVINGS] [NUT FREE, NO OIL] Tortillas stand in for homemade crust here, making these mouthwatering turnovers easy to prepare. As a child I loved apple turnovers, and this recipe (surprisingly) truly mimics the taste of this childhood favorite . . . with a jazzy twist, of course!

---

1 medium apple, peeled, cored, and diced
4 teaspoons maple syrup
¼ teaspoon ground cinnamon
4 6-inch whole-grain flour tortillas (see note)
Vegan confectioners' sugar, for dusting

CHEF'S NOTE

You may use 8- or 9-inch tortillas for this recipe. If you do, use a large apple or 2 small apples for the filling.

Preheat the oven to 375 degrees F. Line a medium, rimmed baking sheet with unbleached parchment paper.

Put the apple, 2 teaspoons maple syrup, and cinnamon in a small mixing bowl and stir until evenly coated. Put a tortilla on a large dinner plate. Brush each side of the tortilla evenly with ¼ teaspoon maple syrup. Spoon one-quarter of the apple mixture into the center of the tortilla. Fold the tortilla over the apple mixture and firmly press the outer edges of the tortilla together to form a tight seal. Decorate the edges and help to further seal the turnover by pressing the tines of a table fork firmly around the outer rim of the turnover. Repeat with the other three tortillas. Put the turnovers on the lined baking sheet and bake for 20 minutes.

Put the sheet on a wire rack. Dust liberally with confectioners' sugar. Cool 10 to 15 minutes and serve warm.

Luscious Apple Tart with Blueberry Glaze

[MAKES 6 SERVINGS] [NUT FREE] Using a whole-grain tortilla for the crust makes this delightful tart easily doable for a weeknight dessert. This delectable beauty makes an impressive dinner-party finale, too, because it looks and tastes just like a fancy French tart! If you'd like to make it gluten-free, a brown rice tortilla works nicely.

1 tablespoon vegan margarine
2 tablespoons maple syrup
1 large whole-grain or brown rice tortilla
1 tablespoon brown sugar or maple sugar
3 small (or 2 large) apples, peeled, cored, and thinly sliced
1 teaspoon ground cinnamon
2 tablespoons blueberry preserves
1 teaspoon filtered or spring water, plus more as needed

Preheat the oven to 375 degrees F. Line a baking sheet with unbleached parchment paper.

Heat the vegan margarine in a small sauce pan over medium-low heat until it melts. Put the melted vegan margarine and maple syrup in a small mixing bowl and stir together to incorporate. Put the tortilla on a large dinner plate. Brush ½ tablespoon of the maple mixture on each side of the tortilla.

Sprinkle ½ tablespoon sugar on the prepared baking sheet. Place the tortilla on top of the sugar. Sprinkle ½ tablespoon sugar evenly over the top of the tortilla.

Put the apples, remaining maple syrup mixture, and cinnamon in a medium mixing bowl. Toss well to coat. Arrange the apples on the tortilla in a spiral fashion, slightly overlapping them. Cover the entire top of the tortilla with the apples in this fashion. Bake for 25 to 30 minutes, or until the apples are soft and edges of tortilla are golden. Put the baking sheet on a wire rack.

Meanwhile, put the blueberry preserves and water in a small mixing bowl and whisk together.

Add more water, ½ teaspoon at a time, if the preserves seem too thick to spread. Spread the preserves evenly over the top of the piping hot tart using a pastry brush or small spoon.

Let the tart cool for 20 minutes. Transfer to a cutting board, cut in wedges, and serve. The tart may be served warm or at room temperature.

Peanut Butter Mousse Tartlets

[MAKES 12 SERVINGS] Peanut butter has never been yummier than when it is piped into these pretty little fruit-and-seed mini-crusts. These creamy, chewy, and crusty gems are the ideal choice to round out any elegant meal.

---

12 large Medjool dates, pitted and chopped
½ cup unsalted, raw sunflower seeds
⅔ cup cubed firm regular tofu (sprouted variety is preferred)
4 tablespoons creamy peanut butter
4 tablespoons maple syrup
12 vegan chocolate chips

CHEF'S NOTE

If you do not have a pastry bag, simply spoon the filling into the cups. Not quite as fancy, but still jazzylicious!

Put the dates and sunflower seeds in a high-performance blending appliance and process to a smooth dough. Put the date mixture in a medium bowl and pull it together to form a ball. Divide the date mixture into 12 parts and roll each into a ball.

Press each ball into the shape of a cup, one at a time, using the cups in a mini-muffin baking tin as a guide. Using an offset spatula or table knife, carefully remove the date cups from the mini-muffin molds, and place them on a flat tray or plate that has been lined with parchment paper.

Put the tofu, peanut butter, and maple syrup in a blender and process until very smooth. Spoon the mixture into a pastry bag fitted with a large star pastry tip (see note). Pipe the filling into each of the date cups and top each with a single vegan chocolate chip.

Cover and refrigerate for 5 to 6 hours before serving. Covered tightly and stored in the refrigerator, leftover tartlets will keep up to 24 hours.

Banana-Raspberry Sorbet

[MAKES 2 SERVINGS] [NUT FREE, NO OIL] This refreshing sorbet whips up in just a few minutes in your blender. This fabulous frozen treat makes the perfect close to any festive summer meal!

2 very large frozen bananas
1 cup frozen raspberries
⅔ cup cold vanilla-flavored nondairy milk, plus more as needed
2 tablespoons maple syrup, plus more, as needed

Put all of the ingredients in a blender. Process slowly, adding more nondairy milk, 1 tablespoon at a time, until incorporated. Process on medium-high speed until mixture has the consistency of a thick sorbet. Taste and add more maple syrup, if desired. Serve immediately in pretty parfait glasses or dessert bowls.

Mango Sorbet

[MAKES 4 SERVINGS] [NUT FREE, NO OIL] I adore serving homemade sorbet because it has a fresh taste not found in store-bought varieties. Frozen mangos give this sorbet a lovely color and a cool, tangy taste.

2 to 3 mangos, peeled, cubed, and frozen
2 to 3 tablespoons maple syrup, plus more as needed
¼ cup filtered or spring water, plus more as needed

Put all of the ingredients in a blender. Process until the mixture resembles a frosty sorbet consistency, adding more water or maple syrup, 1 tablespoon at a time, as needed to achieve the desired consistency. Serve immediately.

Mango Sorbet

About the Author

Laura Theodore is a popular television personality and radio host, vegan chef, compassionate cookbook author, and award-winning jazz singer and actor. She is the proud creator of the Jazzy Vegetarian brand and author of *Jazzy Vegetarian: Lively Vegan Cuisine Made Easy and Delicious*.

Laura is the on-camera host, writer, and co-producer of the *Jazzy Vegetarian* cooking show on public television. In addition, she hosts the weekly radio show, *Jazzy Vegetarian Radio*, a talk/music format focusing on plant-based recipes, eco-friendly tips, celebrity interviews, and upbeat music, served up with a bit of fun on the side.

Laura has made guest appearances on ABC, NBC, CBS, and Public Television, and she has been featured on *The Insider*, *Entertainment Tonight* online, News 4-NBC, Better TV, and CBS Radio. Laura has been featured in the *New York Times*, *USA Today*, *New York Daily News*, *New York Post*, VegNews, *Family Circle*, *Readers Digest*, PBS Food, and *Time* magazine, among others.

As a jazz singer and songwriter, Laura has recorded six solo CDs, including her Musician Magazine Award–winning album, *Tonight's the Night*. Her CD release with the late, great Joe Beck, entitled *Golden Earrings*, was selected to appear on the 52nd Grammy Awards list in the category of Best Jazz Vocal Album. Laura has appeared in more than sixty musicals, including the hit off-Broadway show *Beehive*, which earned her a coveted Backstage Bistro Award. She was honored with the Denver Drama Critics Circle Award as Best Actress in a Musical for her starring role as Janis Joplin in the world premiere production of *Love, Janis*.

A love for good food, compassion for animals, and enthusiasm for great music has created a joyous life path for Laura Theodore.

Connect with Jazzy Vegetarian online

JazzyVegetarian.com

🐦 @JazzyVegetarian

f Facebook.com/JazzyVegetarian

Index